DEPARTMENT OF THE TREASURY
TECHNICAL EXPLANATION OF THE CONVENTION AND PROTOCOL BETWEEN
THE GOVERNMENT OF THE UNITED STATES OF AMERICA
AND
THE GOVERNMENT OF THE REPUBLIC OF VENEZUELA
FOR THE AVOIDANCE OF DOUBLE TAXATION AND
THE PREVENTION OF FISCAL EVASION
WITH RESPECT TO TAXES ON INCOME AND CAPITAL

INTRODUCTION

This document is a technical explanation of the Convention and Protocol between the United States and Venezuela that was signed at Caracas on January 25, 1999 (the "Convention"). Negotiations took into account the U.S. Treasury Department's current tax treaty policy, as reflected in the U.S. Treasury Department's Model Income Tax Convention of September 20, 1996 (the "U.S. Model") and its recently negotiated tax treaties, the Model Income Tax Convention on Income and on Capital, published by the OECD in 1992 and amended in 1994, 1995 and 1997 (the "OECD Model"), and recent tax treaties concluded by Venezuela.

The Technical Explanation is an official guide to the Convention. It reflects the policies behind particular Convention provisions, as well as understandings reached with respect to the application and interpretation of the Convention. References in the Technical Explanation to "he" or "his" should be read to mean "he or she" and "his or her."

ARTICLE 1 (GENERAL SCOPE)

Paragraph 1

Paragraph 1 of Article 1 provides that the Convention applies to residents of the United States or Venezuela except where the terms of the Convention provide otherwise. Under Article 4 (Residence) a person is generally treated as a resident of a Contracting State if that person is, under the laws of that State, liable to tax therein by reason of his domicile, a period of physical presence, or other similar criteria. If, however, a person is considered a resident of both Contracting States, Article 4 provides rules for determining a single state of residence (or no state of residence). This determination governs for all purposes of the Convention.

Certain provisions are applicable to persons who may not be residents of either Contracting State. For example, Article 20 (Government Service) may apply to an employee of a Contracting State who is resident in neither State. Likewise, under Article 27 (Exchange of Information), information may be exchanged with respect to residents of third states. Also, paragraph 1 of Article 25 (Non-Discrimination) applies to nationals of the Contracting States.

Paragraph 2

Paragraph 2 states the generally accepted relationship both between the Convention and domestic law and between the Convention and other agreements between the Contracting States (i.e., that no provision in the Convention may restrict any exclusion, exemption, deduction, credit or other allowance or benefit accorded by the tax laws of the Contracting States, or by any other agreement between the Contracting States). The list in paragraph 2 contains examples of benefits not to be restricted and is not intended to be exhaustive.

For example, if a deduction would be allowed under the U.S. Internal Revenue Code (the "Code") in computing the U.S. taxable income of a resident of Venezuela, the deduction also is allowed to that person in computing taxable income under the Convention. Paragraph 2 also means that the Convention may not increase the tax burden on a resident of a Contracting State beyond the burden determined under domestic law. Thus, a right to tax given by the Convention cannot be exercised unless that right also exists under internal law. The relationship between the non-discrimination provisions of the Convention and other agreements is not addressed in paragraph 2 but in paragraph 3.

It follows that under the principle of paragraph 2, a taxpayer's liability to U.S. tax need not be determined under the Convention if the Code would produce a more favorable result. A taxpayer may not, however, choose among the provisions of the Code and the Convention in an inconsistent manner in order to minimize tax. For example, assume that a resident of Venezuela has three separate businesses in the United States. One is a profitable permanent establishment and the other two are trades or businesses that would earn taxable income under the Code but that do not meet the permanent establishment threshold tests of the Convention. One is profitable and the other incurs a loss. Under the Convention, the income of the permanent establishment is taxable, and both the profit and loss of the other two businesses are ignored. Under the Code, all three would be subject to tax, but the loss would be offset against the profits of the two profitable ventures. The taxpayer may not invoke the Convention to exclude the profits of the profitable trade or business and invoke the Code to claim the loss of the trade or business against the profit of the permanent establishment. (See, Rev. Rul. 84-17, 1984-1 C.B. 308.) If, however, the taxpayer invokes the Code for the taxation of all three ventures, he would not be precluded from invoking the Convention with respect, for example, to any dividend income he may receive from the United States that is not effectively connected with any of his business activities in the United States.

Similarly, nothing in the Convention can be used to deny any benefit granted by any other agreement between the United States and Venezuela. For example, if certain benefits are provided for diplomats under a Consular Convention between the United States and Venezuela, those benefits or protections will be available to residents of the Contracting States regardless of any provisions to the contrary (or silence) in the Convention.

DEPARTMENT OF THE TREASURY
TECHNICAL EXPLANATION OF THE CONVENTION AND PROTOCOL BETWEEN
THE GOVERNMENT OF THE UNITED STATES OF AMERICA
AND
THE GOVERNMENT OF THE REPUBLIC OF VENEZUELA
FOR THE AVOIDANCE OF DOUBLE TAXATION AND
THE PREVENTION OF FISCAL EVASION
WITH RESPECT TO TAXES ON INCOME AND CAPITAL

Paragraph 3

Paragraph 3 specifically relates to non-discrimination obligations of the Contracting States under other agreements. The provisions of paragraph 3 are an exception to the rule provided in paragraph 2 of this Article under which the Convention shall not restrict in any manner any benefit now or hereafter accorded by any other agreement between the Contracting States.

Subparagraph (a) of paragraph 3 provides that, notwithstanding any other agreement to which the Contracting States may be parties, a dispute concerning whether a measure is within the scope of this Convention shall be considered only by the competent authorities of the Contracting States, and the procedures under this Convention exclusively shall apply to the dispute. Thus, procedures for dealing with disputes that may be incorporated into trade, investment, or other agreements between the Contracting States shall not apply for the purpose of determining the scope of the Convention.

Subparagraph (b) of paragraph 3 provides that, unless the competent authorities determine that a taxation measure is not within the scope of this Convention, the non-discrimination obligations of this Convention exclusively shall apply with respect to that measure, except for such national treatment or most-favored-nation ("MFN") obligations as may apply to trade in goods under the General Agreement on Tariffs and Trade ("GATT"). No national treatment or MFN obligation under any other agreement shall apply with respect to that measure. Thus, unless the competent authorities agree otherwise, any national treatment and MFN obligations undertaken by the Contracting States under agreements other than the Convention shall not apply to a taxation measure, with the exception of GATT as applicable to trade in goods.

Subparagraph (c) of paragraph 3 defines a "measure" broadly. It would include, for example, a law, regulation, rule, procedure, decision, administrative action or guidance, or any other form of governmental action or guidance.

Paragraph 4

Paragraph 4 contains the traditional saving clause found in U.S. treaties. The Contracting States reserve their rights, except as provided in paragraph 5, to tax their residents and citizens as provided in their internal laws, notwithstanding any provisions of the Convention to the contrary. For example, if a resident of Venezuela performs independent personal services in the United States and the income from the services is not attributable to a fixed base in the United States, Article 14 (Independent Personal Services) would by its terms prevent the United States from taxing the income. If, however, the resident of Venezuela is also a citizen of the United States, the saving clause permits the United States to include the remuneration in the worldwide income of the citizen and subject it to tax under the normal Code rules (i.e., without regard to Code section 894(a)).

For purposes of the saving clause, "residence" is determined under Article 4 (Residence). Thus, if an individual who is not a U.S. citizen is a resident of the United States under the Code, and is also a resident of Venezuela under its law, and that individual has a permanent home available to him in Venezuela and not in the United States, he would be treated as a resident of Venezuela under Article 4 and for purposes of the saving clause. The United States would not be permitted to apply its statutory rules to that person if they are inconsistent with the treaty. Thus, an individual who is a U.S. resident under the Internal Revenue Code but who is deemed to be a resident of Venezuela under the tie-breaker rules of Article 4 (Residence) would be subject to U.S. tax only to the extent permitted by the Convention. However, the person would be treated as a U.S. resident for U.S. tax purposes other than determining the individual's U.S. tax liability. For example, in determining under Code section 957 whether a foreign corporation is a controlled foreign corporation, shares in that corporation held by the individual would be considered to be held by a U.S. resident. As a result, other U.S. citizens or residents might be deemed to be United States shareholders of a controlled foreign corporation subject to current inclusion of Subpart F income recognized by the corporation. See, Treas. Reg. section 301.7701(b)-7(a)(3).

Paragraph 1 of the Protocol clarifies that for purposes of the saving clause, the term "citizens" in paragraph 4 includes former U.S. citizens whose loss of citizenship had, as one of its principal purposes, the avoidance of tax. The United States treats an individual as having a principal purpose to avoid tax if (a) the average annual net income tax of such individual for the period of 5 taxable years ending before the date of the loss of status is greater than $100,000, or (b) the net worth of such individual as of such date is $500,000 or more. In the United States, such a former citizen is taxable in accordance with the provisions of section 877 of the Code.

Section 877 of the Code also provides that the United States may likewise tax its former long-term residents whose loss of such long-term residence had as one of its principal purposes the avoidance of tax. The United States' right to tax those former long-term residents is preserved in the saving clause of the U.S. Model. This Convention, however, achieves this result with the inclusion of paragraph 3 of Article 17 (Limitation on Benefits), which denies these individuals the benefits of the Convention. The United States defines "long-term resident" as an individual (other than a U.S. citizen) who is a lawful permanent resident of the United States in at least 8 of the prior 15 taxable years. An individual shall not be treated as a lawful permanent resident for any taxable year if such individual is treated as a resident of a foreign country under the provisions of a tax treaty between the United States and the foreign country and the individual does not waive the benefits of such treaty applicable to residents of the foreign country.

Paragraph 5

Some provisions are intended to provide benefits to citizens and residents even if such benefits do not exist under internal law. Paragraph 5 sets forth certain exceptions to the saving clause that preserve these benefits for citizens and residents of the Contracting States. Sub-paragraph (a) lists certain provisions of the Convention that are applicable to all citizens and residents of a Contracting State, despite the general saving clause rule of paragraph 4: (1) Paragraph 2 of Article 9 (Associated Enterprises) grants the right to a correlative adjustment with respect to income tax due on profits reallocated under Article 9. (2) Article 24 (Relief from Double Taxation) confirms the benefit of a credit, exemption or other relief from double taxation to citizens and residents of one Contracting State for income taxes paid to the other. (3) Article 25 (Non-Discrimination) requires one Contracting State to grant national treatment to residents and citizens of the other Contracting State in certain circumstances. Excepting this Article from the saving clause requires, for example, that the United States give such benefits to a resident or citizen of Venezuela even if that person is a citizen of the United States. (4) Article 26 (Mutual Agreement Procedure) may confer benefits on citizens and residents of the Contracting States. For example, the statute of limitations may be waived for refunds and the competent authorities are permitted to use a definition of a term that differs from the internal law definition. As with the foreign tax credit, these benefits are intended to be granted by a Contracting State to its citizens and residents.

Subparagraph (b) of paragraph 5 provides a different set of exceptions to the saving clause. The benefits referred to are all intended to be granted to temporary residents of a Contracting State (for example, in the case of the United States, holders of non-immigrant visas), but not to citizens or to persons who have acquired permanent residence in that State. If beneficiaries of these provisions travel from one of the Contracting States to the other, and remain in the other long enough to become residents under its internal law, but do not acquire permanent residence status (i.e., in the U.S. context, they do not become "green card" holders) and are not citizens of that State, the host State will continue to grant these benefits even if they conflict with the statutory rules. The benefits preserved by this paragraph are the host country exemptions for the following items: tax treatment of government service salaries and pensions under Article 20 (Government Service); certain income of visiting students and trainees under Article 21 (Students, Trainees, Teachers and Researchers); and the income of diplomatic agents and consular officers under Article 28 (Diplomatic Agents and Consular Officers).

ARTICLE 2 (TAXES COVERED)

This Article specifies the U.S. taxes and the Venezuelan taxes to which the Convention applies. Unlike Article 2 in the OECD Model, but consistent with the U.S. Model format, this Article does not contain a general description of the types of taxes that are covered (i.e., income taxes), but only a listing of the specific taxes covered for both of the Contracting States. With three exceptions, the taxes specified in Article 2 are the covered taxes for all purposes of the Convention. A broader coverage applies for purposes of Articles 25 (Non-Discrimination) and 27 (Exchange of Information). Article 25 applies with respect to all taxes, including those imposed by state and local governments. Article 27 applies with respect to all taxes imposed at the national level. Article 24 (Relief from Double Taxation) provides narrower coverage in that while Venezuela's business assets tax (BAT) is a covered tax, the United States is not required by the Convention to grant a U.S. foreign tax credit for business assets taxes paid to Venezuela.

Paragraph 1

Subparagraph (a) provides that the Venezuelan covered taxes are Venezuela's income tax and its business assets tax (amplified as described above in the cases of Articles 25 (Non-Discrimination) and (Exchange of Information)). Coverage of the business assets tax limits its imposition to cases where a U.S. resident either (i) has a permanent establishment in Venezuela under Article 5, (ii) has real property in Venezuela, or (iii) leases or otherwise permits a resident of Venezuela to use property for which a "royalty" (as defined in Article 12) is paid. The United States is not required, under Article 24 (Relief from Double Taxation) to grant a foreign tax credit for assets taxes paid to Venezuela.

Subparagraph (b) provides that the United States covered taxes are the Federal income taxes imposed by the Code. Although they may be regarded as income taxes, social security taxes (Code sections 1401, 3101, 3111 and 3301) are specifically excluded from coverage. It is expected that social security taxes will be dealt with in bilateral Social Security Totalization Agreements, which are negotiated and administered by the Social Security Administration. Except with respect to Article 25 (Non-Discrimination), state and local taxes in the United States are not covered by the Convention.

In this Convention, unlike some U.S. treaties, the Accumulated Earnings Tax and the Personal Holding Companies Tax are covered taxes because they are income taxes and they are not otherwise excluded from coverage. Under the Code, these taxes will not apply to most foreign corporations because of a statutory exclusion or the corporation's failure to meet a statutory requirement.

Paragraph 2

Under paragraph 2, the Convention will apply to any taxes that are identical, or substantially similar, to those enumerated in paragraph 1, and which are imposed in addition to, or in place of, the existing taxes after the date of signature of the Convention. The paragraph also provides that the competent authorities of the Contracting States will notify each other of significant changes in their taxation laws that affect their obligations under the Convention. The use of the term "significant" means that changes must be reported that are of significance to the operation of the Convention. The competent authorities are also obligated to notify each other of official published materials concerning the application of the Convention.

ARTICLE 3 (GENERAL DEFINITIONS)

Paragraph 1

Paragraph 1 defines a number of basic terms used in the Convention. Certain others are defined in other articles of the Convention. For example, the term "resident of a Contracting State" is defined in Article 4 (Residence). The term "permanent establishment" is defined in Article 5 (Permanent Establishment). The terms "dividends," "interest" and "royalties" are defined in Articles 10, 11 and 12, respectively. The introduction to paragraph 1 makes clear that these definitions apply for all purposes of the Convention, unless the context requires otherwise. This latter condition allows flexibility in the interpretation of the treaty in order to avoid unintended results. Terms that are not defined in the Convention are dealt with in paragraph 2.

The term "Venezuela" is defined in subparagraph (a) to mean the Republic of Venezuela.

The term "United States" is defined in subparagraph (b) to mean the United States of America, which includes the territorial seas of the United States, but not including Puerto Rico, the Virgin Islands, Guam or any other United States possession or territory.

Paragraph 3 of the Protocol further provides that, only for purposes of this Convention and when referred to in a geographical sense, "Venezuela" and "United States" include the areas of the seabed and subsoil adjacent to their respective territorial seas in which they may exercise rights in accordance with domestic legislation and with international law. This extension applies to the extent that the United States or Venezuela exercises sovereignty in accordance with domestic legislation and with international law for the purpose of natural resource exploration and exploitation of such areas. This extension of the definition applies, however, only if the person, property or activity to which the Convention is being applied is connected with such natural resource exploration or exploitation. Thus, for example, the extension would not include any activity involving the sea floor of an area over which the United States exercised sovereignty for natural resource purposes if that activity was unrelated to the exploration and exploitation of natural resources.

Subparagraph 1 (c) defines the terms "Contracting State" and "the other Contracting State" as meaning Venezuela or the United States depending on the context in which the term is used. That is, a provision using the terms "Contracting State" and "other Contracting State" is bilateral, and "Contracting State" may be interpreted, as necessary, to be either Venezuela or the United States.

Subparagraph 1(d) defines the term "person" to include an individual, a trust, a partnership, a company and any other body of persons. The definition of "person" is significant for a variety of reasons. For example, under Article 4, only a "person" can be a "resident" and therefore eligible for most benefits under the treaty. Also, all "persons" are eligible to claim relief under Article 26 (Mutual Agreement Procedure).

Although are not expressly listed in subparagraph 1 (d), Venezuelan *"entidades"* and *"colectividades"*, as defined under Article 22.3 of Venezuela's Organic Tax Code (*Código Orgánico Tributario*), shall, for the purposes of this Convention, be included within the term "person". These entities, while not legal persons under Venezuelan law, are nevertheless taxable persons under the taxation laws of Venezuela. Therefore, it was agreed that they should be included within the definitions of "person," as well as "national," and "resident" (the latter subject to the Limitation on Benefits provisions of the Convention). In accordance with paragraph 2 of Article 3, the meaning of the terms "partnership," "trust" and "estate" is to be determined by reference to the law of the Contracting State whose tax is being applied.

The term "company" is defined in subparagraph (e) as a body corporate or an entity treated as a body corporate for tax purposes. Although the Convention does not add "in the State in which it is organized," as does the U.S. Model, the result should be the same, as the Commentaries to the OECD Model interpret the language identical to that of the Convention in a manner consistent with the U.S. Model.

The terms "enterprise of a Contracting State" and "enterprise of the other Contracting State" are defined in subparagraph (f) as an enterprise carried on by a resident of a Contracting State and an enterprise carried on by a resident of the other Contracting State. The term "enterprise" is not defined in the Convention, nor is it defined in the OECD Model or its Commentaries. Despite the absence of a clear, generally accepted meaning for the term "enterprise," the term is understood to refer to any activity or set of activities that constitute a trade or business.

Like the U.S. Model, subparagraph (f) provides that these terms also encompass an enterprise conducted through an entity (such as a partnership) that is treated as fiscally transparent in the Contracting State where the entity's owner is resident. This phrase has been included in the Convention in order to address more explicitly some of the problems presented by fiscally transparent entities. In accordance with Article 4 (Residence), entities that are fiscally transparent in the country in which their owners are resident are not considered to be residents of a Contracting State (although income derived by such entities may be taxed as the income of a resident, if taxed in the hands of resident partners or other owners). Given the approach taken in Article 4, an enterprise conducted by such an entity arguably could not qualify as an enterprise of a Contracting State under the OECD Model because the OECD definition of enterprise requires that the enterprise be conducted by a resident, although most countries would attribute the enterprise to the owners of the entity in such circumstances. The definition in the Convention is intended to make clear that an enterprise conducted by such an entity will be treated as carried on by a resident of a Contracting State to the extent its partners or other owners are residents. This approach is consistent with the Code, which under section 875 attributes a trade or business conducted by a partnership to its partners and a trade or business conducted by an estate or trust to its beneficiaries.

An enterprise of a Contracting State need not be carried on in that State. It may be carried on in the other Contracting State or a third state (e.g., a U.S. corporation doing all of its business in Venezuela would still be a U.S. enterprise).

The term "national," as it relates to the United States and to Venezuela, is defined in subparagraphs 1(g)(i) and (ii). This term is relevant for purposes of Articles 4 (Residence), 20 (Government Service) and 25 (Non-discrimination). A national of one of the Contracting States is (1) an individual possessing the nationality of that State, and (2) any legal person, association or other entity (including an *"entidad"* or *"colectividad"*) deriving its status as such from the law in force in the State where it is established. This definition is closely analogous to that found in the OECD Model.

The inclusion of juridical persons in the definition may have significance in relation to paragraph 1 of Article 25 (Non-discrimination), which provides that nationals of one Contracting State may not be subject in the other to any taxes or connected requirements that are other or more burdensome than those applicable to nationals of that other State who are in the same circumstances.

Subparagraph 1(h) defines the term "international operation of ships or aircraft." The term means any transport by a ship or aircraft except when the transport is solely between places within a Contracting State. This definition is applicable principally in the context of Article 8 (Shipping and Air Transport), which refers to "operation of ships or aircraft in international traffic", which is to be understood to have the same meaning as "international operation of ships or aircraft". The definition in the OECD Model refers to the operator of the ship or aircraft having its place of effective management in a Contracting State (i.e., being a resident of that State). This Convention does not include that limitation. The broader definition combines with paragraphs 2 and 3 of Article 8 to exempt from tax by the source State income from the rental of ships, aircraft or containers that is earned both by lessors that are operators of ships and aircraft and by those lessors that are not (e.g., banks or container leasing companies).

The exclusion from the definition of "international operation of ships or aircraft" of transport solely between places within a Contracting State means, for example, that carriage of goods or passengers solely between New York and Chicago would not be treated as the international operation of ships or aircraft, whether carried by a U.S. or a foreign carrier. The substantive taxing rules of the Convention relating to the taxation of income from transport, principally Article 8 (Shipping and Air Transport), therefore, would not apply to income from such carriage. Thus, if the carrier engaged in internal U.S. traffic were a resident of Venezuela (assuming that were possible under U.S. law), the United States would not be required to exempt the income from that transport under Article 8. The income would, however, be treated as business profits under Article 7 (Business Profits), and therefore would be taxable in the United States only if attributable to a U.S. permanent establishment of the foreign carrier, and then only on a net basis. The gross basis U.S. tax imposed by section 887 would never apply under the circumstances described. If, however, goods or passengers are carried by a carrier resident in Venezuela from a non-U.S. port to, for example, New York, and some of the goods or passengers continue on to Chicago, the entire transport would be international traffic. This would be true if the international carrier transferred the goods at the U.S. port of entry from a ship to a land vehicle, from a ship to a lighter, or even if the overland portion of the trip in the United

States was handled by an independent carrier under contract with the original international carrier, so long as both parts of the trip were reflected in original bills of lading. For this reason, the Convention refers, in the definition of "international operation of ships or aircraft," to "such transport" being solely between places in the other Contracting State, while the OECD Model refers to the ship or aircraft being operated solely between such places. The Convention's definition is intended to make clear that, as in the above example, even if the goods are carried on a different aircraft for the internal portion of the international voyage than is used for the overseas portion of the trip, the definition applies to that internal portion as well as the external portion.

Finally, a "cruise to nowhere," i.e., a cruise beginning and ending in a port in the same Contracting State with no stops in a foreign port, would not constitute international traffic.

Subparagraphs 1(i)(i) and (ii) define the term "competent authority" for the United States and Venezuela, respectively. The U.S. competent authority is the Secretary of the Treasury or his delegate. The Secretary of the Treasury has delegated the competent authority function to the Commissioner of Internal Revenue, who in turn has delegated the authority to the Assistant Commissioner (International). With respect to interpretative issues, the Assistant Commissioner acts with the concurrence of the Associate Chief Counsel (International) of the Internal Revenue Service. The Venezuelan competent authority is the Integrated National Service of Tax Administration (*Servicio Nacional Integrado de Administración Tributaria -- SENIAT*), its authorized representative or the authority which is designated by the Ministry of Finance as competent authority.

Paragraph 2

Paragraph 2 provides that in the application of the Convention, any term used but not defined in the Convention will have the meaning that it has under the law of the Contracting State whose tax is being applied, unless the context requires otherwise. Finally, there also may be cases where the tax laws of a State contain multiple definitions of the same term. In such a case, the definition used for purposes of the particular provision at issue, if any, should be used.

If the meaning of a term cannot be readily determined under the law of a Contracting State, or if there is a conflict in meaning under the laws of the two States that creates difficulties in the application of the Convention, the competent authorities, as indicated in paragraph 3(e) of Article 26 (Mutual Agreement Procedure), may establish a common meaning in order to prevent double taxation or to further any other purpose of the Convention. This common meaning need not conform to the meaning of the term under the laws of either Contracting State.

It is understood that the reference in paragraph 2 to the internal law of a Contracting State means the law in effect at the time the treaty is being applied, not the law as in effect at the time the treaty was signed. Even before its explicit inclusion in the U.S. Model, this use of "ambulatory definitions" was implicitly understood in previous U.S. and OECD Models.

The use of an ambulatory definition, however, may lead to results that are at variance with the intentions of the negotiators and of the Contracting States when the treaty was negotiated and ratified. The reference in both paragraphs 1 and 2 to the "context otherwise requiring" a definition different from the treaty definition, in paragraph 1, or from the internal law definition of the Contracting State whose tax is being imposed, under paragraph 2, refers to a circumstance where the result intended by the Contracting States is different from the result that would obtain under either the paragraph 1 definition or the statutory definition. Thus, flexibility in defining terms is necessary and permitted.

ARTICLE 4 (RESIDENCE)

This Article sets forth rules for determining whether a person is a resident of a Contracting State for purposes of the Convention. As a general matter, only residents of the Contracting States may claim the benefits of the Convention. The treaty definition of residence is to be used only for purposes of the Convention. The fact that a person is determined to be a resident of a Contracting State under Article 4 does not necessarily entitle that person to the benefits of the Convention. In addition to being a resident, a person also must qualify for benefits under Article 17 (Limitation on Benefits) in order to receive benefits conferred on residents of a Contracting State.

The determination of residence for treaty purposes looks first to a person's liability to tax as a resident under the respective taxation laws of the Contracting States. As a general matter, a person who, under those laws, is a resident of one Contracting State and not of the other need look no further. For purposes of the Convention, that person is a resident of the State in which he is resident under internal law. If, however, a person is resident in both Contracting States under their respective taxation laws, the Article proceeds, where possible, to use tie-breaker rules to assign a single State of residence to such a person for purposes of the Convention.

Paragraph 1

The term "resident of a Contracting State" is defined in paragraph 1. Due to differences in the structures of the United States and Venezuelan tax systems, paragraph 1 establishes particular definitions of resident for each country. Subparagraph (a) provides the definition applicable to the United States. It is based generally on the definitions of residence in U.S. law by referring to a resident as a person who, under the laws of the United States, is subject to tax there by reason of his domicile, residence, citizenship, place of management, place of incorporation or any other similar criterion. Thus, residents of the United States include aliens who are considered U.S. residents under Code section 7701(b).

Subparagraph (a) also provides that a U.S. citizen or alien lawfully admitted for permanent residence in the United States (i.e., a "green card" holder) who is not, under subparagraph 1 (b), a resident of Venezuela, will be treated as a resident of the United States for purposes of the Convention, and, thereby entitled to treaty benefits, only if he has a permanent home or habitual abode in the United States. If, however, such an individual is a resident both of the United States and Venezuela under the rules of paragraph 1, whether he is to be treated as a resident of the United States or of Venezuela for purposes of the Convention is determined by the tie-breaker rules of paragraph 4 of the Article, regardless of how close his nexus to the United States may be. Thus, for example, an individual resident of Mexico who is a U.S. citizen by birth, or who is a Mexican citizen and holds a U.S. green card, but who, in either case, has never lived in the United States, would not be entitled to Venezuelan benefits under the Convention. On the other hand, a U.S. citizen employed by a U.S. corporation who is transferred to Mexico for two years but who maintains a permanent home or habitual abode in the United States would be entitled to treaty benefits. However, the fact that a U.S. citizen who does not have close ties to the United States may not be treated as a U.S. resident under the Convention does not alter the application of the saving clause of paragraph 4 of Article 1 (General Scope) to that citizen. For example, a U.S. citizen who pursuant to the "citizen/green card holder" rule is not considered to be a resident of the United States still is taxable on his worldwide income under the generally applicable rules of the Code.

Subparagraph (b) provides the definition of resident applicable to Venezuela and reflects Venezuela's domestic law definitions of taxable residents. The subparagraph provides that residence for individuals is based on the concept of the *"domiciliado."* An individual is considered a *domiciliado,* and therefore a resident of Venezuela in a given tax year for purposes of the Convention, if he is present in Venezuela for more than 180 days in that tax year or in the preceding year. Subparagraph (b) also provides that any legal person that is created or organized under the laws of Venezuela shall be considered a resident of Venezuela. This provision reflects Venezuela's domestic law definition of corporate residence, which is analogous to the place-of-incorporation rule used in the United States. Any corporation registered under a commercial registry in Venezuela (i.e., incorporated in Venezuela) is considered a taxable resident for domestic law purposes and, under this subparagraph, for purposes of the Convention. The subparagraph also provides explicit inclusion as residents of those Venezuelan *entidades* and *colectividades* that are subject to the taxation applicable to corporations, which is necessary because those entities are not legal bodies incorporated in Venezuela. Those *entidades* and *colectividades* not taxed as corporations are fiscally transparent in Venezuela, and are therefore subject to the provision of paragraph 2 of this Article.

Certain entities that are nominally subject to tax but that in practice rarely pay tax also would generally be treated as residents and therefore accorded treaty benefits. For example, RICs, REITs and REMICs are all residents of the United States for purposes of the treaty. Although the income earned by these entities normally is not subject to U.S. tax in the hands of the entity, they are taxable to the extent that they do not currently distribute their profits, and therefore may be regarded as "liable to tax." They also must satisfy a number of requirements under the Code in order to be entitled to special tax treatment.

The Protocol's paragraph 3 describes additional entities which are to be considered residents for purposes of the Convention. Protocol paragraph 3 is analogous to subparagraphs 1 (b) and 1 (c) of the U.S. Model's Article 4. Subparagraph 3 (a) makes clear the generally understood practice of including within the term "resident of a Contracting State" the Government of that state as well as any political subdivisions or local authorities, agencies and other instrumentalities of that State.

Subparagraph 3 (b) of the Protocol corresponds to the U.S. Model's Article 4 paragraph 1 (b) and provides that certain tax-exempt entities such as pension funds and charitable organizations will be regarded as residents regardless of whether they are generally liable for income tax in the State where they are established. An entity will be described in this subparagraph if it is generally exempt from tax by reason of the fact that it is organized and operated exclusively to perform a charitable or similar purpose or to provide pension benefits to employees.

The inclusion of this provision is intended to clarify the generally accepted practice of treating an entity that would be liable for tax as a resident under the internal law of a State but for a specific exemption from tax (either complete or partial) as a resident of that State for purposes of paragraph 1. The reference to a general exemption is intended to reflect the fact that under U.S. law, certain organizations that generally are considered to be tax-exempt entities may be subject to certain excise taxes or to income tax on their unrelated business income. Thus, a U.S. pension trust, or an exempt section 501(c) organization (such as a U.S. charity) that is generally exempt from tax under U.S. law is considered a resident of the United States for all purposes of the treaty.

Paragraph 2

Paragraph 2 addresses special issues presented by fiscally transparent entities such as partnerships and certain estates and trusts. This paragraph applies to any resident of a Contracting State who is entitled to income derived through an entity that is treated as fiscally transparent under the laws of either Contracting State. Entities falling under this description in the United States would include partnerships, common investment trusts under section 584 and grantor trusts. This paragraph also applies to U.S. limited liability companies ("LLCs") that are treated as partnerships for U.S. tax purposes.

Paragraph 2 provides that an item of income derived by such a fiscally transparent entity will be considered to be derived by a resident of a Contracting State if the resident is treated under the taxation laws of the State where he is resident as deriving the item of income. For example, if a corporation resident in Venezuela distributes a dividend to an entity that is treated as fiscally transparent for U.S. tax purposes, the dividend will be considered derived by a resident of the United States only to the extent that the taxation laws of the United States treat one or more U.S. residents (whose status as U.S. residents is determined, for this purpose, under U.S. tax laws) as deriving the dividend income for U.S. tax purposes. In the case of a partnership, the persons who are, under U.S. tax laws, treated as partners of the entity would normally be the persons whom the U.S. tax laws would treat as deriving the dividend income through the partnership. Thus, it also follows that persons whom the United States treats as partners but who are not U.S. residents for U.S. tax purposes may not claim a benefit for the dividend paid to the entity under the Convention. Although these partners are treated as deriving the income for U.S. tax purposes, they are not residents of the United States for purposes of the treaty. If, however, they are treated as residents of a third country under the provisions of an income tax convention which that country has with Venezuela, they may be entitled to claim a benefit under that convention. In contrast, if an entity is organized under U.S. laws and is classified as a corporation for U.S. tax purposes, dividends paid by a corporation resident in Venezuela to the U.S. entity will be considered derived by a resident of the United States since the U.S. corporation is treated under U.S. taxation laws as a resident of the United States and as deriving the income.

These results would obtain even if the entity were viewed differently under the tax laws of Venezuela (e.g., as not fiscally transparent in the first example above where the entity is treated as a partnership for U.S. tax purposes or as fiscally transparent in the second example where the entity is viewed as not fiscally transparent for U.S. tax purposes). These results also follow regardless of where the entity is organized, i.e., in the United States, Venezuela, or in a third country. For example, income from sources in Venezuela received by an entity organized under the laws of Venezuela, which is treated for U.S. tax purposes as a corporation and is owned by a U.S. shareholder who is a U.S. resident for U.S. tax purposes, is not considered derived by the shareholder of that corporation even if, under the tax laws of Venezuela, the entity is treated as fiscally transparent. Rather, for purposes of the treaty, the income is treated as derived by an entity resident in Venezuela. These results also follow regardless of whether the entity is disregarded as a separate entity under the laws of one jurisdiction but not the other, such as a single owner entity that is viewed as a branch for U.S. tax purposes and as a corporation for tax purposes of the other Contracting State.

The taxation laws of a Contracting State may treat an item of income, profit or gain as income, profit or gain of a resident of that State even if, under the taxation laws of that State, the resident is not subject to tax on that particular item of income, profit or gain. For example, U.S.-source dividends would be regarded as income or gain of a resident of Venezuela who otherwise derived the income or gain, despite the fact that the resident could be exempt from tax in Venezuela on the dividend because of Venezuela's territorial system of taxation.

Where income is derived through an entity organized in a third state that has owners resident in one of the Contracting States, the characterization of the entity in that third state is irrelevant for purposes of determining whether the resident is entitled to treaty benefits with respect to income derived by the entity.

These principles also apply to trusts to the extent that they are fiscally transparent in either Contracting State. For example, if X, a resident of Venezuela, creates a revocable trust and names persons resident in a third country as the beneficiaries of the trust, X would be treated as the beneficial owner of income derived from the United States under the Code's rules. If Venezuela has no rules comparable to those in sections 671 through 679 then it is possible that under that State's law neither X nor the trust would be taxed on the income derived from the United States. In these cases paragraph 2 provides that the trust's income would be regarded as being derived by a resident of Venezuela only to the extent that the laws of Venezuela treat residents of Venezuela as deriving the income for tax purposes.

Paragraph 3

If, under the laws of the two Contracting States, and, thus, under paragraph 1, an individual is deemed to be a resident of both Contracting States, a series of tie-breaker rules are provided in paragraph 3 to determine a single State of residence for that individual. These tests are to be applied in the order in which they are stated. The first test is based on where the individual has a permanent home. If that test is inconclusive because the individual has a permanent home available to him in both States, he will be considered to be a resident of the Contracting State where his personal and economic relations are closest (i.e., the location of his "center of vital interests"). If that test is also inconclusive, or if he does not have a permanent home available to him in either State, he will be treated as a resident of the Contracting State where he maintains an habitual abode. If he has an habitual abode in both States or in neither of them, he will be treated as a resident of the Contracting State of which he is a national. If he is a national of both States or of neither, the matter will be considered by the competent authorities, who will attempt to agree to assign a single State of residence.

Paragraph 4

Dual residents other than individuals (such as companies, trusts or estates) are addressed by paragraph 4. If such a person is, under the rules of paragraph 1, resident in both Contracting States, the competent authorities shall seek to reach a mutual agreement in determining a single State of residence for that person for purposes of the Convention. If the competent authorities are unable to reach such an agreement, the dual-resident person shall not be considered a resident of either Contracting State, and shall therefore not be granted the benefits of the Convention. Since it is only for the purposes of deriving treaty benefits that such dual residents are excluded from the Convention, they may be treated as resident for other purposes. For example, if a dual resident corporation pays a dividend to a resident of Venezuela, the U.S. withholding agent would be permitted to withhold on that dividend at the appropriate treaty rate, since reduced withholding is a benefit enjoyed by the resident of Venezuela receiving the dividend, not by the dual resident. The dual resident corporation that pays the dividend would, for this purpose, be treated as a resident of the United States under the Convention.

ARTICLE 5 (PERMANENT ESTABLISHMENT)

This Article defines the term "permanent establishment," a term that is significant for several articles of the Convention. The existence of a permanent establishment in a Contracting State is necessary under Article 7 (Business Profits) for the taxation by that State of the business profits of a resident of the other Contracting State. Since the term "fixed base" in Article 14 (Independent Personal Services) is understood by reference to the definition of "permanent establishment," this Article is also relevant for purposes of Article 14. Articles 10, 11 and 12 (dealing with dividends, interest, and royalties, respectively) provide for reduced rates of tax at source on payments of these items of income to a resident of the other State only when the income is not attributable to a permanent establishment or fixed base that the recipient has in the source State. The concept is also relevant in determining which Contracting State may tax certain gains under Article 13 (Gains) and certain "other income" under Article 22 (Other Income).

Paragraph 1

The basic definition of the term "permanent establishment" is contained in paragraph 1. As used in the Convention, the term means a fixed place of business through which the business of an enterprise is wholly or partly carried on. As indicated in the OECD Commentaries (see paragraphs 4 through 8), a general principle to be observed in determining whether a permanent establishment exists is that the place of business must be "fixed" in the sense that a particular building or physical location is used by the enterprise for the conduct of its business, and that it must be foreseeable that the enterprise's use of this building or other physical location will be more than temporary.

Paragraph 2

Paragraph 2 lists a number of types of fixed places of business that constitute a permanent establishment. This list is illustrative and non-exclusive. According to paragraph 2, the term permanent establishment includes a place of management, a branch, an office, a factory, a workshop, and a mine, oil or gas well, quarry or other place of extraction of natural resources.

Paragraph 3

Paragraph 3 describes several additional activities of business sites that will constitute a permanent establishment. Paragraph 3 (a) provides rules to determine whether a building site or a construction, assembly or installation project, or an installation or drilling rig or ship used for the exploration of natural resources constitutes a permanent establishment for the contractor, driller, etc. An activity does not create a permanent establishment unless the site, project, etc. lasts or continues for more than 183 days within any twelve month period commencing or ending in the taxable year concerned. It is only necessary to refer to "exploration" and not "exploitation" in this context because exploitation activities are defined to constitute a permanent establishment under subparagraph (f) of paragraph 2. Thus, a drilling rig does not constitute a permanent establishment if a well is drilled in only three months. However, if production begins in the following month, the well becomes a permanent establishment as of that date. As explained in subparagraph (b) of paragraph 4 of the Protocol, unlike the OECD Model, the time period calculation under the Convention shall not take into account time spent solely on preparatory activities, such as obtaining permits.

The 183 day test applies separately to each site or project. The 183 day period begins when work physically begins in a Contracting State. A series of contracts or projects by a contractor that are interdependent both commercially and geographically are to be treated as a single project for purposes of applying the 183 day threshold test. For example, the construction of a housing development would be considered as a single project even if each house were constructed for a different purchaser. Several drilling rigs operated by a drilling contractor in the same sector of the continental shelf also normally would be treated as a single project.

If the 183 day threshold is exceeded, the site or project constitutes a permanent establishment from the first day of activity. Subparagraph (a) of paragraph 4 of the Protocol clarifies that in applying paragraph 3, time spent by a sub-contractor on a building site shall be counted as time spent by the general contractor at the site for purposes of determining whether the general contractor has a permanent establishment. However, for the sub-contractor itself to be treated as having a permanent establishment, the sub-contractor's activities at the site must last for more than 183 days within any twelve month period commencing or ending in the taxable year concerned. If a sub-contractor is on a site intermittently, then, for purposes of applying the 183-day rule, time is measured from the first day the sub-contractor is on the site until the last day (i.e., intervening days that the sub-contractor is not on the site are counted).

These interpretations of the Article are based on the Commentary to paragraph 3 of Article 5 of the OECD Model and are consistent with the generally accepted international interpretation of the relevant language in paragraph 3 of Article 5 of the Convention.

The paragraph also specifies, in subparagraph (b), that the furnishing of services in a Contracting State by an enterprise either through employees or others engaged for that purpose will constitute a permanent establishment, so long as the activities continue physically in that State for a period or periods aggregating more than 183 days within any twelve month period commencing or ending in the taxable year concerned.

Paragraph 4

This paragraph contains exceptions to the general rule of paragraph 1, listing a number of activities that may be carried on through a fixed place of business, but which nevertheless do not create a permanent establishment. The use of facilities solely to store, display or deliver merchandise belonging to an enterprise, does not constitute a permanent establishment of that enterprise. The maintenance of a stock of goods belonging to an enterprise solely for the purpose of storage, display or delivery, or solely for the purpose of processing by another enterprise does not give rise to a permanent establishment of the first-mentioned enterprise. The maintenance of a fixed place of business solely for the purpose of purchasing goods or merchandise, or for collecting information, for the enterprise, or for other activities that have a preparatory or auxiliary character for the enterprise, such as advertising, or the supply of information, do not constitute a permanent establishment of the enterprise. Thus, as explained in paragraph 22 of the OECD Commentaries, a news bureau of a newspaper would not constitute a permanent establishment of the newspaper.

Subparagraph (f) provides that the maintenance of a fixed place of business for a combination of the activities listed in subparagraphs (a) through (e) of the paragraph does not give rise to a permanent establishment. The Convention contains the OECD Model's qualification that the overall combination of activities must be of a preparatory or auxiliary character. As further clarified in paragraph 5 of the Protocol, the maintaining of sales personnel in a Contracting State would not be an activity excepted under paragraph 4 and, if the requirements of paragraphs 1,5 and 6 of Article 5 are met, would constitute a permanent establishment.

Paragraph 5

Paragraphs 5 and 6 specify when activities carried on by an agent on behalf of an enterprise create a permanent establishment of that enterprise. Under paragraph 5, a dependent agent of an enterprise is deemed to be a permanent establishment of the enterprise if the agent has and habitually exercises an authority to conclude contracts that are binding on the enterprise. If, however, the agent's activities are limited to those activities specified in paragraph 4 which would not constitute a permanent establishment if carried on by the enterprise through a fixed place of business, the agent is not a permanent establishment of the enterprise.

The Convention uses the OECD Model term "in the name of that enterprise" rather than the U.S. Model term "binding on the enterprise". There is no substantive difference. As indicated in paragraph 32 to the OECD Commentaries on Article 5, the application of the provision is not limited to "an agent who enters into contracts literally in the name of the enterprise; the paragraph applies equally to an agent who concludes contracts which are binding on the enterprise, even if those contracts are not actually in the name of the enterprise."

The contracts referred to in paragraph 5 are those relating to the essential business operations of the enterprise, rather than ancillary activities. For example, if the agent has no authority to conclude contracts in the name of the enterprise with its customers for, say, the sale of the goods produced by the enterprise, but it can enter into service contracts in the name of the enterprise for the enterprise's business equipment used in the agent's office, this contracting authority would not fall within the scope of the paragraph, even if exercised regularly.

Paragraph 6

Under paragraph 6, an enterprise is not deemed to have a permanent establishment in a Contracting State merely because it carries on business in that State through an independent agent, including a broker or general commission agent, if the agent is acting in the ordinary course of his business. Thus, there are two conditions that must be satisfied: the agent must be both legally and economically independent of the enterprise, and the agent must be acting in the ordinary course of its business in carrying out activities on behalf of the enterprise.

Whether the agent and the enterprise are independent is a factual determination. Among the questions to be considered are the extent to which the agent operates on the basis of instructions from the enterprise. An agent that is subject to detailed instructions regarding the conduct of its operations or comprehensive control by the enterprise is not legally independent.

In determining whether the agent is economically independent, a relevant factor is the extent to which the agent bears business risk. Business risk refers primarily to risk of loss. An independent agent typically bears risk of loss from its own activities. In the absence of other factors that would establish dependence, an agent that shares business risk with the enterprise, or has its own business risk, is economically independent because its business activities are not integrated with those of the principal. Conversely, an agent that bears little or no risk from the activities it performs is not economically independent and therefore is not described in paragraph 6.

Another relevant factor in determining whether an agent is economically independent is whether the agent has an exclusive or nearly exclusive relationship with the principal. Such a relationship may indicate that the principal has economic control over the agent. A number of principals acting in concert also may have economic control over an agent. The limited scope of the agent's activities and the agent's dependence on a single source of income may indicate that the agent lacks economic independence. The paragraph provides that an agent will be considered a permanent establishment of an enterprise (under Paragraph 5) when the activities of that agent are devoted wholly or almost wholly on behalf of that enterprise, and the conditions between the agent and the enterprise differ from those which would be made between independent persons (i.e., the agent and the enterprise are not operating at arms length).

It should be borne in mind, however, that in the absence of transactions between the agent and the enterprise under non-arm's length conditions, exclusivity is not in itself a conclusive test: an agent may be economically independent notwithstanding an exclusive relationship with the principal if it has the capacity to diversify and acquire other clients without substantial modifications to its current business and without substantial harm to its business profits. Thus, exclusivity should be viewed merely as a pointer to further investigation of the relationship between the principal and the agent. Each case must be addressed on the basis of its own facts and circumstances.

Paragraph 7

This paragraph clarifies that a company that is a resident of a Contracting State is not deemed to have a permanent establishment in the other Contracting State merely because it controls, or is controlled by, a company that is a resident of that other Contracting State, or that carries on business in that other Contracting State. The determination whether a permanent establishment exists is made solely on the basis of the factors described in paragraphs 1 through 6 of the Article. Whether a company is a permanent establishment of a related company, therefore, is based solely on those factors and not on the ownership or control relationship between the companies.

ARTICLE 6 (INCOME FROM IMMOVABLE PROPERTY (REAL PROPERTY))

Paragraph 1

This paragraph states the general rule that income of a resident of a Contracting State derived from real property situated in the other Contracting State may be taxed in the Contracting State in which the property is situated. Paragraph 1 specifies that income from immovable property (real property) includes income from agriculture and forestry. Income from agriculture and forestry are dealt with in Article 6 rather than in Article 7 (Business Profits). Given the availability of the net election in paragraph 5 for those taxpayers who, under the domestic law of the situs State, are not otherwise allowed to compute their tax on income from real property on a net basis, taxpayers generally should be able to obtain the same tax treatment in the situs country regardless of whether the income is treated as business profits or real property income. Paragraph 3 clarifies that the income referred to in paragraph 1 also means income from any use of real property, including, but not limited to, income from direct use by the owner (in which case income may be imputed to the owner for tax purposes) and rental income from the letting of real property.

This Article does not grant an exclusive taxing right to the situs State; the situs State is merely given the primary right to tax. The Article does not impose any limitation in terms of rate or form of tax on the situs State, except that, as provided in paragraph 5, the situs State must allow the taxpayer an election to be taxed on a net basis if such treatment is not otherwise available under domestic law.

Paragraph 2

The term "immovable property (real property)" is defined in paragraph 2 mainly by reference to the internal law definition in the situs State. In the case of the United States, the term has the meaning given to it by Reg. 1.897-1(b). In addition to the statutory definitions in the two Contracting States, the paragraph specifies certain additional classes of property that, regardless of internal law definitions, are to be included within the meaning of the term for purposes of the Convention. This expanded definition conforms to that in the OECD Model. The definition of "immovable property (real property)" for purposes of Article 6 is more limited than the expansive definition of "immovable property (real property)" situated in the other Contracting State" in paragraphs 1 and 2 of Article 13 (Capital Gains). The Article 13 term includes not only immovable property as defined in Article 6 but certain other interests in real property.

Paragraph 3

Paragraph 3 makes clear that all forms of income derived from the exploitation of real property are taxable in the Contracting State in which the property is situated. In the case of a net lease of real property, if the domestic law of the Contracting State levying the tax does not tax this income on a net basis, and if in that case, a net taxation election has not been made as provided in paragraph 5, the gross rental payment (before deductible expenses incurred by the lessee) is treated as income from the property.

Income from the disposition of an interest in real property is not considered "derived" from real property and is not dealt with in Article 6. The taxation of that income is addressed in Article 13 (Gains). Also, the interest paid on a mortgage on real property and distributions by a U.S. Real Estate Investment Trust are not dealt with in Article 6. Such payments would fall under Articles 10 (Dividends), 11 (Interest) or 13 (Gains). Finally, dividends paid by a United States Real Property Holding Corporation are not considered to be income from the exploitation of real property: such payments would fall under Article 10 (Dividends) or 13(Gains).

Paragraph 4

This paragraph specifies that the basic rule of paragraph 1 (as elaborated in paragraph 3) applies to income from real property of an enterprise and to income from real property used for the performance of independent personal services. This clarifies that the situs country may tax the real property income (including rental income) of a resident of the other Contracting State in the absence of attribution to a permanent establishment or fixed base in the situs State. This provision represents an exception to the general rule under Articles 7 (Business Profits) and 14 (Independent Personal Services) that income must be attributable to a permanent establishment or fixed base, respectively, in order to be taxable in the situs State.

Paragraph 5

This paragraph provides that a resident of one Contracting State who is liable to tax on real property income situated in the other Contracting State and who is not otherwise allowed to compute the tax on such income on a net basis may elect, for any taxable year, to be subject to tax in that other State on a net basis, as though the income were attributable to a permanent establishment in that other State. The election may be terminated with the consent of the competent authority of the situs State. In the United States, revocation will be granted in accordance with the provisions of Treas. Reg. section 1.871-10(d)(2).

ARTICLE 7 (BUSINESS PROFITS)

This Article provides rules for the taxation by a Contracting State of the business profits of an enterprise of the other Contracting State.

Paragraph 1

Paragraph 1 states the general rule that business profits of an enterprise of one Contracting State may not be taxed by the other Contracting State unless the enterprise carries on business in that other Contracting State through a permanent establishment (as defined in Article 5 (Permanent Establishment)) situated there. When that condition is met, the State in which the permanent establishment is situated may tax the enterprise, but only on a net basis and only on the income that is attributable to the permanent establishment. This paragraph is identical to paragraph 1 of Article 7 of the OECD Model.

Paragraph 2

Paragraph 2 provides rules for the attribution of business profits to a permanent establishment. The Contracting States will attribute to a permanent establishment the profits that it would have earned had it been an independent enterprise engaged in the same or similar activities under the same or similar circumstances. This language incorporates the arm's-length standard for purposes of determining the profits attributable to a permanent establishment. The computation of business profits attributable to a permanent establishment under this paragraph is subject to the rules of paragraph 4 and paragraph 6 of the Protocol for the allowance of allocation of expenses incurred for the purposes of earning the profits.

The "attributable to" concept of paragraph 2 is analogous but not entirely equivalent to the "effectively connected" concept in Code section 864(c). The profits attributable to a permanent establishment may be from sources within or without a Contracting State.

This Article does not contain a provision corresponding to paragraph 4 of Article 7 of the OECD Model. That paragraph provides that a Contracting State in certain circumstances may determine the profits attributable to a permanent establishment on the basis of an apportionment of the total profits of the enterprise. Any such approach, however, must be designed to approximate an arm's length result. This paragraph has not been included in the Convention because it is unnecessary. The U.S. view is that paragraphs 2 and 3 of Article 7 authorize the use of such approaches independently of paragraph 4 of Article 7 of the OECD Model because total profits methods are acceptable methods for determining the arm's length profits of associated enterprises under Article 9 (Associated Enterprises). Accordingly, it is understood that, under paragraph 2 of the Convention, it is permissible to use methods other than separate accounting to determine the arm's length profits of a permanent establishment where it is necessary to do so for practical reasons, such as when the affairs of the permanent establishment are so closely bound up with those of the head office that it would be impossible to disentangle them on any strict basis of accounts.

Paragraph 3

Paragraph 3 provides that nothing in this Article shall affect the application of any law of a Contracting State relating to the determination of the tax liability of any person in cases where the information available to the competent authority of that State is inadequate to determine the profits to be attributed to a permanent establishment. The Internal Revenue Service would have this power even in the absence of such a specific provision. In any such case, however, determination of the profits of the permanent establishment must be consistent with the principles stated in this Article (i.e., it must seek to reflect arm's length pricing and appropriate deductions of expenses.

Paragraph 4

This paragraph is in substance the same as paragraph 3 of Article 7 of the OECD Model, although it is more detailed. Paragraph 4 provides that in determining the business profits of a permanent establishment, deductions shall be allowed for the expenses incurred for the purposes of the permanent establishment, ensuring that business profits will be taxed on a net basis. This rule is not limited to expenses incurred exclusively for the purposes of the permanent establishment, but includes, as clarified in paragraph 6 of the Protocol, a reasonable allocation of expenses incurred for the purposes of the enterprise as a whole, or that part of the enterprise that includes the permanent establishment. Deductions are to be allowed regardless of which accounting unit of the enterprise books the expenses, so long as they are incurred for the purposes of the permanent establishment. For example, a portion of the interest expense recorded on the books of the home office in one State may be deducted by a permanent establishment in the other if properly allocable thereto.

Paragraph 4 clarifies, as does the UN Model and the commentary to the OECD Model, that a permanent establishment may not take any deduction for royalties, fees, commissions, or service fees paid to its home office or other office of the enterprise other than amounts which represent reimbursement of actual expenses incurred by such office. Since the permanent establishment and the home and other offices of the enterprise are parts of a single entity, there should be no profit element in such intra-company transfers. Similarly, a permanent establishment may not increase its business profits by the amount of any notional fees for ancillary services performed for another unit of the enterprise, but also should not receive a deduction for the expense of providing such services, since those expenses would be incurred for purposes of a business unit other than the permanent establishment.

The last sentence of paragraph 4, which is neither in the U.S. Model nor in the OECD Model, allows each Contracting State, consistent with its law, to impose limitations on the deductions taken by the permanent establishment as long as the limitations are consistent with the concept of net income. This sentence is intended to be only a clarification, and does not alter the definition of allowable deductions in the U.S. and OECD Models. It would not permit the Contracting States to deny a deduction for wages or interest expenses since such expenses are so fundamental that denial of deductions would be inconsistent with the concept of net income.

Paragraph 6 of the Protocol specifies that the expenses that may be considered to be incurred for the purposes of the permanent establishment are expenses for research and development, interest and other similar expenses, as well as a reasonable amount of executive and general administrative expenses. This paragraph also explains that these deductions shall be allowed, regardless of where they are incurred, but only to the extent that they have not been deducted by the enterprise, and have not been reflected in other deductions allowed to the permanent establishment, such as deductions for the cost of goods sold or of the purchases. The allocation of expenses must be accomplished in a manner that reflects to a reasonably close extent the factual relationship between the deduction and the permanent establishment and the enterprise. Some examples of bases and factors that can be used in allocating expenses according to this factual relationship are provided in paragraph 6 of the Protocol, and are taken from the bases and factors described in Temporary Treas. Reg. § 1.861-8T(c)(1). Accordingly, this rule permits (but does not require) each Contracting State to apply the type of expense allocation rules provided by U.S. law (such as in Treas. Reg. §§ 1.861-8 and 1.882-5).

Paragraph 5

Paragraph 5 provides that no business profits can be attributed to a permanent establishment merely because it purchases goods or merchandise for the enterprise of which it is a part. This rule applies only to an office that performs functions for the enterprise in addition to purchasing. The income attribution issue does not arise if the sole activity of the permanent establishment is the purchase of goods or merchandise because such activity does not give rise to a permanent establishment under Article 5 (Permanent Establishment). A common situation in which paragraph 5 is relevant is one in which a permanent establishment purchases raw materials for the enterprise's manufacturing operation conducted outside the United States and sells the manufactured product. While business profits may be attributable to the permanent establishment with respect to its sales activities, no profits are attributable to it with respect to its purchasing activities.

Paragraph 6

Paragraph 6 provides that the business profits attributed to a permanent establishment include only those profits derived from that permanent establishment's assets or activities. This rule is consistent with the "asset-use" and "business activities" test of Code section 864(c)(2). The OECD Model does not expressly provide such a limitation, although it generally is understood to be implicit in paragraph 1 of Article 7 of the OECD Model. This provision was included in the Convention to make it clear that the limited force of attraction rule of Code section 864(c)(3) is not incorporated into paragraph 2.

This paragraph also tracks paragraph 6 of Article 7 of the OECD Model, providing that profits shall be determined by the same method each year, unless there is good reason to change the method used. This rule assures consistent tax treatment over time for permanent establishments. It limits the ability of both the Contracting State and the enterprise to change accounting methods to be applied to the permanent establishment. It does not, however, restrict a Contracting State from imposing additional requirements, such as the rules under Code section 481, to prevent amounts from being duplicated or omitted following a change in method.

Paragraph 7

Paragraph 7 coordinates the provisions of Article 7 and other provisions of the Convention. Under this paragraph, when business profits include items of income that are dealt with separately under other articles of the Convention, the provisions of those articles will, except when they specifically provide to the contrary, take precedence over the provisions of Article 7. For example, the taxation of dividends will be determined by the rules of Article 10 (Dividends), and not by Article 7, except where, as provided in paragraph 6 of Article 10, the dividend is attributable to a permanent establishment or fixed base. In the latter case the provisions of Articles 7 or 14 (Independent Personal Services) apply. Thus, an enterprise of one State deriving dividends from the other State may not rely on Article 7 to exempt those dividends from tax at source if they are not attributable to a permanent establishment of the enterprise in the other State. By the same token, if the dividends are attributable to a permanent establishment in the other State, the dividends may be taxed on a net income basis at the source State's full corporate tax rate, rather than on a gross basis under Article 10 (Dividends).

As provided in Article 8 (Shipping and Air Transport), income derived from shipping and air transport activities in international traffic described in that Article is taxable only in the country of residence of the enterprise regardless of whether it is attributable to a permanent establishment situated in the source State.

Paragraph 8

Paragraph 8 incorporates into the Convention the rule of Code section 864(c)(6). Like the Code section on which it is based, paragraph 8 provides that any income or gain attributable to a permanent establishment or a fixed base during its existence is taxable in the Contracting State where the permanent establishment or fixed base is situated, even if the payment of that income or gain is deferred until after the permanent establishment or fixed base ceases to exist. This rule applies with respect to paragraphs 1 and 2 of Article 7 (Business Profits), paragraph 6 of Article 10 (Dividends), paragraph 6 of Article 11 (Interest), paragraph 4 of Article 12 (Royalties), paragraph 3 of Article 13 (Gains), Article 14 (Independent Personal Services) and paragraph 2 of Article 22 (Other Income).

The effect of this rule can be illustrated by the following example. Assume a company that is a resident of Venezuela and that maintains a permanent establishment in the United States winds up the permanent establishment's business and sells the permanent establishment's inventory and assets to a U.S. buyer at the end of year 1 in exchange for an interest-bearing installment obligation payable in full at the end of year 3. Despite the fact that Article 13's threshold require-ment for U.S. taxation is not met in year 3 because the company has no permanent establishment in the United States, the United States may tax the deferred income payment recognized by the company in year 3.

Relation to other articles

This Article is subject to the saving clause of paragraph 4 of Article 1 (General Scope). Thus, if a citizen of the United States who is a resident of Venezuela under the treaty derives business profits from the United States that are not attributable to a permanent establishment in the United States, the United States may tax those profits, notwithstanding the provision of paragraph 1 of this Article which would exempt the income from U.S. tax.

The benefits of this Article are also subject to Article 17 (Limitation on Benefits). Thus, an enterprise of the other Contracting State that derives income effectively connected with a U.S. trade or business may not claim the benefits of Article 7 unless the resident carrying on the enterprise qualifies for such benefits under Article 17.

ARTICLE 8 (SHIPPING AND AIR TRANSPORT)

This Article governs the taxation of profits from the international operation of ships and aircraft. Paragraph 7 of the Protocol makes clear that the provisions of this Article shall not affect the continued validity of the Agreement Between the Government of the United States and the Government of the Republic of Venezuela For The Avoidance of Double Taxation With Respect to Shipping and Air Transport, signed December 29, 1987, in Caracas, Venezuela. The taxation of gains from the alienation of ships, aircraft or containers is not dealt with in this Article but in paragraph 4 of Article 13 (Gains).

Paragraph 1

Paragraph 1 provides that profits derived by an enterprise of a Contracting State from the operation in international traffic of ships or aircraft are taxable only in that Contracting State. Because paragraph 7 of Article 7 (Business Profits) defers to Article 8 with respect to shipping income, such income derived by a resident of one of the Contracting States may not be taxed in the other State even if the enterprise has a permanent establishment in that other State. Thus, if a U.S. airline has a ticket office in Venezuela, Venezuela may not tax the airline's profits attributable to that office under Article 7. Since entities engaged in international transportation activities normally will have many permanent establishments in a number of countries, the rule avoids difficulties that would be encountered in attributing income to multiple permanent establishments if the income were covered by Article 7 (Business Profits).

Paragraph 2

The income from the operation of ships or aircraft in international traffic that is exempt from tax under paragraph 1 is defined in paragraph 2.

In addition to income derived directly from the operation of ships and aircraft in international traffic, this definition also includes certain items of rental income that are closely related to those activities. First, income of an enterprise of a Contracting State from the rental of ships or aircraft on a full basis (i.e., with crew) when such ships or aircraft are used in international traffic is income of the lessor from the operation of ships and aircraft in international traffic and, therefore, is exempt from tax in the other Contracting State under paragraph 1. Also, paragraph 2 encompasses income from the lease of ships or aircraft on a bareboat basis (i.e., without crew), either when the ships or aircraft are operated in international traffic by the lessee, or when the income is incidental to other income of the lessor from the operation of ships or aircraft in international traffic. As discussed above, of these classes of rental income, only non-incidental, bareboat lease income is not covered by Article 8 of the OECD Model. The scope of Article 8 is thus the same as the U.S. Model, but broader than that of the OECD Model as it covers rentals from bareboat leasing that are not incidental to the operation of ships or aircraft by the resident itself.

Paragraph 2 also clarifies, consistent with the Commentary to Article 8 of the OECD Model, that income earned by an enterprise from the inland transport of property or passengers within either Contracting State falls within Article 8 if the transport is undertaken as part of the international transport of property or passengers by the enterprise. Thus, if a U.S. shipping company contracts to carry property from Venezuela to a U.S. city and, as part of that contract, it transports the property by truck from its point of origin to an airport in Venezuela (or it contracts with a trucking company to carry the property to the airport) the income earned by the U.S. shipping company from the overland leg of the journey would be taxable only in the United States. Similarly, Article 8 also would apply to income from lighterage undertaken as part of the international transport of goods.

Finally, certain non-transport activities that are an integral part of the services performed by a transport company are understood to be covered in paragraph 1, though they are not specified in paragraph 2. These include, for example, the performance of some maintenance or catering services by one airline for another airline, if these services are incidental to the provision of those services by the airline for itself. Income earned by concessionaires, however, is not covered by Article 8. These interpretations of paragraph 1 also are consistent with the Commentary to Article 8 of the OECD Model.

Paragraph 3

Under this paragraph, profits of an enterprise of a Contracting State from the use, maintenance or rental of containers (including equipment for their transport) that are used for the transport of goods in international traffic are exempt from tax in the other Contracting State. This result obtains under paragraph 3 regardless of whether the recipient of the income is engaged in the operation of ships or aircraft in international traffic, and regardless of whether the enterprise has a permanent establishment in the other Contracting State. By contrast, Article 8 of the OECD Model covers only income from the use, maintenance or rental of containers that is incidental to other income from international traffic.

Paragraph 4

This paragraph clarifies that the provisions of paragraphs 1 and 3 also apply to profits derived by an enterprise of a Contracting State from participation in a pool, joint business or international operating agency. This refers to various arrangements for international cooperation by carriers in shipping and air transport. For example, airlines from two countries may agree to share the transport of passengers between the two countries. They each will fly the same number of flights per week and share the revenues from that route equally, regardless of the number of passengers that each airline actually transports. Paragraph 4 makes clear that with respect to each carrier the income dealt with in the Article is that carrier's share of the total transport, not the income derived from the passengers actually carried by the airline.

Relation to other articles

As with other benefits of the Convention, the benefit of exclusive residence country taxation under Article 8 is available to an enterprise only if it is entitled to benefits under Article 22 (Limitation on Benefits).

This Article also is subject to the saving clause of paragraph 4 of Article 1 (General Scope) of the Model. Thus, if a citizen of the United States who is a resident of Venezuela derives profits from the operation of ships or aircraft in international traffic, notwithstanding the exclusive residence country taxation in paragraph 1 of Article 8, the United States may tax those profits as part of the worldwide income of the citizen. (This is an unlikely situation, however, because non-tax considerations (e.g., insurance) generally result in shipping activities being carried on in corporate form.)

ARTICLE 9 (ASSOCIATED ENTERPRISES)

This Article incorporates in the Convention the arm's-length principle reflected in the U.S. domestic transfer pricing provisions, particularly Code section 482. It provides that when related enterprises engage in a transaction on terms that are not arm's-length, the Contracting States may make appropriate adjustments to the taxable income and tax liability of such related enterprises to reflect what the income and tax of these enterprises with respect to the transaction would have been had there been an arm's-length relationship between them.

Paragraph 1

This paragraph addresses the situation where an enterprise of a Contracting State is related to an enterprise of the other Contracting State, and there are arrangements or conditions imposed between the enterprises in their commercial or financial relations that are different from those that would have existed in the absence of the relationship. Under these circumstances, the Contracting States may adjust the income (or loss) of the enterprise to reflect what it would have been in the absence of such a relationship.

The paragraph identifies the relationships between enterprises that serve as a prerequisite to application of the Article. As the Commentary to the OECD Model makes clear, the necessary element in these relationships is effective control, which is also the standard for purposes of section 482. Thus, the Article applies if an enterprise of one State participates directly or indirectly in the management, control, or capital of the enterprise of the other State. Also, the Article applies if any third person or persons participate directly or indirectly in the management, control, or capital of enterprises of different States. For this purpose, all types of control are included, i.e., whether or not legally enforceable and however exercised or exercisable.

The fact that a transaction is entered into between such related enterprises does not, in and of itself, mean that a Contracting State may adjust the income (or loss) of one or both of the enterprises under the provisions of this Article. If the conditions of the transaction are consistent with those that would be made between independent persons, the income arising from that transaction should not be subject to adjustment under this Article.

Similarly, the fact that associated enterprises may have concluded arrangements, such as cost sharing arrangements or general services agreements, is not in itself an indication that the two enterprises have entered into a non-arm's-length transaction that should give rise to an adjustment under paragraph 1. Both related and unrelated parties enter into such arrangements (e.g., joint venturers may share some development costs). As with any other kind of transaction, when related parties enter into an arrangement, the specific arrangement must be examined to see whether or not it meets the arm's-length standard. In the event that it does not, an appropriate adjustment may be made, which may include modifying the terms of the agreement or re-characterizing the transaction to reflect its substance.

It is understood that the "commensurate with income" standard for determining appropriate transfer prices for intangibles, added to Code section 482 by the Tax Reform Act of 1986, was designed to operate consistently with the arm's-length standard. The implementation of this standard in the section 482 regulations is in accordance with the general principles of paragraph 1 of Article 9 of the Convention, as interpreted by the OECD Transfer Pricing Guidelines.

This Article also permits tax authorities to deal with thin capitalization issues. They may, in the context of Article 9, scrutinize more than the rate of interest charged on a loan between related persons. They also may examine the capital structure of an enterprise, whether a payment in respect of that loan should be treated as interest, and, if it is treated as interest, under what circumstances interest deductions should be allowed to the payor. Paragraph 2 of the Commentaries to Article 9 of the OECD Model, together with the U.S. observation set forth in paragraph 15 thereof, sets forth a similar understanding of the scope of Article 9 in the context of thin capitalization.

Paragraph 2

When a Contracting State has made an adjustment that is consistent with the provisions of paragraph 1, and the other Contracting State agrees that the adjustment was appropriate to reflect arm's-length conditions, that other Contracting State is obligated to make a correlative adjustment (sometimes referred to as a "corresponding adjustment") to the tax liability of the related person in that other Contracting State. Although the OECD Model does not specify that the other

Contracting State must agree with the initial adjustment before it is obligated to make the correlative adjustment, the Commentary makes clear that the paragraph is to be read that way.

As explained in the OECD Commentaries, Article 9 leaves the treatment of "secondary adjustments" to the laws of the Contracting States. When an adjustment under Article 9 has been made, one of the parties will have in its possession funds that it would not have had at arm's length. The question arises as to how to treat these funds. In the United States the general practice is to treat such funds as a dividend or contribution to capital, depending on the relationship between the parties. Under certain circumstances, the parties may be permitted to restore the funds to the party that would have the funds at arm's length, and to establish an account payable pending restoration of the funds. See, Rev. Proc. 99-32, 1993-34 I.R.B. 296.

The Contracting State making a secondary adjustment will take the other provisions of the Convention, where relevant, into account. For example, if the effect of a secondary adjustment is to treat a U.S. corporation as having made a distribution of profits to its parent corporation in Venezuela, the provisions of Article 10 (Dividends) will apply, and the United States may impose a 5 percent withholding tax on the dividend. Also, if under Article 23 Venezuela generally exempts such dividends from Venezuelan income tax, it would also be required to do so in this case.

The competent authorities are authorized by paragraph 2 to consult, if necessary, to resolve any differences in the application of these provisions. For example, there may be a disagreement over whether an adjustment made by a Contracting State under paragraph 1 was appropriate.

If a correlative adjustment is made under paragraph 2, it is to be implemented, pursuant to paragraph 2 of Article 25 (Mutual Agreement Procedure), notwithstanding any time limits or other procedural limitations in the law of the Contracting State making the adjustment. If a taxpayer has entered a closing agreement (or other written settlement) with the United States prior to bringing a case to the competent authorities, the U.S. competent authority will endeavor only to obtain a correlative adjustment from the other Contracting State. See, Rev. Proc. 96-13, 1996-13 I.R.B. 31, Section 7.05.

Paragraph 3

Paragraph 3 preserves the rights of the Contracting States to apply internal law provisions relating to adjustments between related parties. They also reserve the right to make adjustments in cases involving tax evasion or fraud. Such adjustments -- the distribution, apportionment, or allocation of income, deductions, credits or allowances -- are permitted even if they are different from, or go beyond, those authorized by paragraph 1 of the Article, as long as they accord with the general principles of paragraph 1, i.e., that the adjustment reflects what would have transpired had the related parties been acting at arm's length. For example, while paragraph 1 explicitly allows adjustments of deductions in computing taxable income, it does not deal with adjustments to tax credits. It does not, however, preclude such adjustments if they can be made under internal law. The provision does not grant authority not otherwise present under internal law. The OECD Model reaches the same result. See paragraph 4 of the Commentaries to Article 9.

Relation to other articles

The saving clause of paragraph 4 of Article 1 (General Scope) does not apply to paragraph 2 of Article 9 by virtue of the exceptions to the saving clause in paragraph 5(a) of Article 1. Thus, even if the statute of limitations has run, a refund of tax can be made in order to implement a correlative adjustment. Statutory or procedural limitations, however, cannot be overridden to impose additional tax, because paragraph 2 of Article 1 provides that the Convention cannot restrict any statutory benefit.

ARTICLE 10 (DIVIDENDS)

Article 10 provides rules for the taxation of dividends paid by a resident of one Contracting State to a beneficial owner that is a resident of the other Contracting State. The article provides for full residence country taxation of such dividends and a limited source State right to tax. Rules for the imposition of a tax on branch profits by the State of source are found in Article 11A (Branch Tax). Finally, the article prohibits a State from imposing a tax on dividends paid by companies resident in the other Contracting State except if such dividends are paid to a resident of the first-mentioned State or are attributable to a permanent establishment or fixed based situated in the first-mentioned State.

Paragraph 1

The right of a shareholder's country of residence to tax dividends arising in the source country is preserved by paragraph 1, which permits a Contracting State to tax its residents on dividends paid to them by a resident of the other Contracting State. For dividends from any other source paid to a resident, Article 22 (Other Income) grants the residence country exclusive taxing jurisdiction, except when the dividends arise in the other State or are attributable to a permanent establishment or fixed base in that other State. In those cases, that other State may also tax the dividend.

Paragraph 2

The State of source may also tax dividends beneficially owned by a resident of the other State, subject to the limitations in paragraph 2. Generally, the source State's tax is limited to 15 percent of the gross amount of the dividend paid. If, however, the beneficial owner of the dividends is a company resident in the other State that holds at least 10 percent of the voting shares of the company paying the dividend, then the source State's tax is limited to 5 percent of the gross amount of the dividend. Indirect ownership of voting shares (through tiers of corporations) and direct ownership of non-voting shares are not taken into account for purposes of determining eligibility for the 5 percent direct dividend rate. Shares are considered voting shares if they provide the power to elect, appoint or replace any person vested with the powers ordinarily exercised by the board of directors of a U.S. corporation.

The benefits of paragraph 2 may be granted at the time of payment by means of reduced withholding at source. It also is consistent with the paragraph for tax to be withheld at the time of payment at full statutory rates, and the treaty benefit to be granted by means of a subsequent refund, so long as such procedures are applied in a reasonable manner.

Paragraph 2 does not affect the taxation of the profits out of which the dividends are paid. The taxation by a Contracting State of the income of its resident companies is governed by the internal law of the Contracting State, subject to the provisions of paragraph 5 of Article 25 (Non-Discrimination).

The term "beneficial owner" is not defined in the Convention, and is, therefore, defined as under the internal law of the country imposing tax (i.e., the source country). The beneficial owner of the dividend for purposes of Article 10 is the person to which the dividend income is attributable for tax purposes under the laws of the source State. Thus, if a dividend paid by a corporation that is a resident of one of the States (as determined under Article 4 (Residence)) is received by a nominee or agent that is a resident of the other State on behalf of a person that is not a resident of that other State, the dividend is not entitled to the benefits of this Article. However, a dividend received by a nominee on behalf of a resident of that other State would be entitled to benefits. These limitations are confirmed by paragraph 12 of the OECD Commentaries to Article 10. See also, paragraph 24 of the OECD Commentaries to Article 1 (General Scope).

Companies holding shares through fiscally transparent entities such as partnerships are considered for purposes of this paragraph to hold their proportionate interest in the shares held by the intermediate entity. As a result, companies holding shares through such entities may be able to claim the benefits of subparagraph (a) under certain circumstances. The lower rate applies when the company's proportionate share of the shares held by the intermediate entity meets the 10 percent voting stock threshold. Whether this ownership threshold is satisfied may be difficult to determine and often will require an analysis of the partnership or trust agreement.

Paragraph 3

Paragraph 3 provides rules that modify the maximum rates of tax at source provided in paragraph 2 in particular cases. The first sentence of paragraph 3 denies the lower direct investment withholding rate of paragraph 2(a) for dividends paid by a U.S. Regulated Investment Company (RIC) or a U.S. Real Estate Investment Trust (REIT). The second sentence states that dividends paid by a RIC will qualify for the 15 percent rate provided by subparagraph 2(b).

The third sentence denies the benefits of both subparagraphs (a) and (b) of paragraph 2 to dividends paid by REITs in certain circumstances, allowing them to be taxed at the U.S. statutory rate (30 percent). The United States limits the source tax on dividends paid by a REIT to the 15 percent rate only when the beneficial owner of the dividend satisfies one or more of three criteria. First, the dividend may qualify if the beneficial owner is an individual resident of the other State who owns not more than 10 percent interest in the REIT. Second, the dividend may qualify for the 15 percent rate if it is paid with respect to a class of stock that is publicly traded and the beneficial owner of the dividends is a person holding an interest of not more than 5 percent of any class of the REIT's stock. Finally, the dividend may qualify for the 15 percent rate if the beneficial owner of the dividend is a person holding an interest of not more than 10 percent of the REIT and the REIT is diversified.

For this purpose, a REIT will be considered diversified if the value of no single interest in the REIT's real property exceeds 10 percent of the REIT's total interests in real property. For purposes of this rule, foreclosure property and mortgages will not be considered an interest in real property unless, in the case of a mortgage, it has substantial equity components. With respect to partnership interests held by a REIT, the REIT will be treated as owning directly the interests in real property held by the partnership.

The denial of the 5 percent withholding rate at source to all RIC and REIT shareholders, and the denial of the 15 percent rate to REIT shareholders that do not meet one of the 3 tests described above, is intended to prevent the use of these entities to gain unjustified source taxation benefits for certain shareholders resident in Venezuela. For example, a corporation resident in the other Contracting State that wishes to hold a diversified portfolio of U.S. corporate shares may hold the portfolio directly and pay a U.S. withholding tax of 15 percent on all of the dividends that it receives. Alternatively, it may acquire a diversified portfolio by purchasing a 10 percent or more of the interests in a RIC. Since the RIC may be a pure conduit, there may be no U.S. tax costs to interposing the RIC in the chain of ownership. Absent the special rule in paragraph 3, such use of the RIC could transform portfolio dividends, taxable in the United States under the Convention at 15 percent, into direct investment dividends taxable only at 5 percent.

Similarly, a resident of Venezuela directly holding U.S. real property would pay U.S. tax either at a 30 percent rate on the gross income or at graduated rates on the net income. As in the preceding example, by placing the real property in a REIT, the investor could transform real estate income into dividend income, taxable at the rates provided in Article 10, significantly reducing the U.S. tax that otherwise would be imposed. This policy avoids a disparity between the taxation of direct real estate investments and real estate investments made through REIT conduits. In the cases covered by the exceptions, the holding in the REIT is not considered the equivalent of a direct holding in the underlying real property.

Paragraph 4

Exemption from tax in the State of source is provided for dividends paid to a beneficial owner that is the other Contracting State, one of its political subdivisions or local authorities. In addition, exemption from tax in the State of source is provided for dividends paid to a beneficial owner that is a governmental entity resident in that other Contracting State constituted and operated exclusively to administer or provide pension benefits. This would include, in the case of the United States, state pension funds organized to provide benefits to retired state employees. In both cases, the exemption shall not apply if the dividends are derived directly or indirectly from the carrying on of a trade or business or from an associated enterprise.

Paragraph 8 of the Protocol provides that the reference in paragraph 4 of Article 10 of the Convention to a "governmental entity constituted and operated exclusively to administer or provide pension benefits" shall include certain public or mixed public and private entities that provide pension benefits. In the case of Venezuela, in order to qualify, such entity must operate under or pursuant to the *Ley del Subsistema de Pensiones* (Law of the Pension System) enacted under the *Ley Orgánica del Sistema de Seguridad Social Integral* (Organic Law of the Integrated Social Security System). The details of that law are described more fully below.

Venezuela is currently considering ways of reforming its government-run social security system. The *Ley del Subsistema de Pensiones*, under or pursuant to which a Venezuelan entity must operate in order to qualify under paragraph 8 of the Protocol, currently is proposed legislation that would replace Venezuela's existing regime with a system of privatized funds, known under the proposed legislation as "individual capitalization funds" which would be permitted to invest in equities. Individuals would open "individual capitalization accounts" that could invest in the individual capitalization fund of the individual's choice. Participation in these accounts would cover all workers. Under the proposed legislation, both the worker and the worker's employer would be required to make contributions to the individual's account. Upon retirement, the worker would receive distributions from his account in amounts based on the account's investment performance. Further, the proposed legislation would establish "intergenerational solidarity funds," for the purpose of providing a guaranteed minimum level of benefits in event of inadequate investment performance of a worker's individual capitalization fund of choice.

The stated objectives of the proposed legislation are to replace the current social security system with a system that retains the fundamental principles of the current system, grant benefits to citizens in general, and avoid inequities that exist between beneficiaries. The proposed legislation contemplates only the "individual capitalization funds" and "intergenerational solidarity funds." Because the system under the proposed legislation is similar, both in its purpose and scope of application to all working Venezuelans and their dependents, to a government-run social security system, the inclusion of the proposed funds within the exemption for dividend payments to certain governmental entities providing pension benefits was judged warranted.

The exemption and the explicit inclusion of the proposed Venezuelan funds is consistent with the policy underlying section 892 of the Code, which provides a general tax exemption for the investment income of foreign governments. Also consistent with that policy, paragraph 4 states that the exemption will not apply if the dividend is derived from the carrying on of commercial activity or if the dividend is paid by an associated enterprise.

Any equivalent U.S. entities would also be eligible to receive the withholding exemption given to such governmental entities. Although the United States currently does not have any such funds, the provision was made reciprocal to ensure that, if the United States were ever to adopt a similar regime, the constituent entities would qualify for benefits.

There is no provision in the OECD Model analogous to paragraph 4 of the Convention.

Because the *Ley del Subsistema de Pensiones* has not been enacted, additional general requirements are listed in paragraph 8 of the Protocol to ensure that the exemption for dividend payments to certain governmental entities providing pension benefits will apply only to entities that operate under or pursuant to a final version of the law that includes the significant features of the proposed law. To satisfy these requirements, the final Venezuelan law must: (1) provide universal coverage; (2) require mandatory contributions by both employers and employees; (3) limit the discretion of the employers and employees to direct investment; (4) restrict distributions or borrowing, directly or indirectly, except upon or until death, retirement or disability; and (5) require that accounts be maintained at only one such qualifying entity at a time. In addition, the entity must be operated, and its investment parameters established, pursuant to governmental oversight and regulation.

Paragraph 5

Paragraph 5 defines the term dividends broadly and flexibly. The definition is intended to cover all arrangements that yield a return on an equity investment in a corporation as determined under the tax law of the state of source, as well as arrangements that might be developed in the future.

The term dividends includes income from shares, or other corporate rights that participate in the profits of the company and are treated as dividends under the laws of the source State. The term also includes income that is subjected to the same tax treatment as income from shares by the law of the State of source. Thus, a constructive dividend that results from a non-arm's length transaction between a corporation and a related party is a dividend. In the case of the United States the term dividend includes amounts treated as a dividend under U.S. law upon the sale or redemption of shares or upon a transfer of shares in a reorganization. See, e.g., Rev. Rul. 92-85, 1992-2 C.B. 69 (sale of foreign subsidiary's stock to U.S. sister company is a deemed dividend to extent of subsidiary's and sister's earnings and profits). Further, a distribution from a U.S. publicly traded limited partnership, which is taxed as a corporation under U.S. law, is a dividend for purposes of Article 10. However, a distribution by a limited liability company is not characterized by the United States as a dividend and, therefore, is not a dividend for purposes of Article 10, provided the limited liability company is not characterized as an association taxable as a corporation under U.S. law. Finally, a payment denominated as interest that is made by a thinly capitalized corporation may be treated as a dividend to the extent that the debt is recharacterized as equity under the laws of the source State.

Paragraph 6

Paragraph 6 excludes from the general source country limitations under paragraph 2 dividends paid with respect to holdings that form part of the business property of a permanent establishment or a fixed base. Such dividends will be taxed on a net basis using the rates and rules of taxation generally applicable to residents of the State in which the permanent establishment or fixed base is located, as modified by the Convention. An example of dividends paid with respect to the business property of a permanent establishment would be dividends derived by a dealer in stock or securities from stock or securities that the dealer held for sale to customers.

In the case of a permanent establishment or fixed base that once existed in the State but that no longer exists, the provisions of paragraph 6 also apply, by virtue of paragraph 8 of Article 7 (Business Profits), to dividends that would be attributable to such a permanent establishment or fixed base if it did exist in the year of payment of accrual. See the Technical Explanation of paragraph 8 of Article 7.

Paragraph 7

A State's right to tax dividends paid by a company that is a resident of the other State is restricted by paragraph 7 to cases in which the dividends are paid to a resident of that State or are attributable to a permanent establishment or fixed base in that State. Thus, a State may not impose a "secondary" withholding tax on dividends paid by a nonresident company out of earnings and profits from that State. In the case of the United States, paragraph 7, therefore, overrides the ability to impose taxes under sections 871 and 882(a) on dividends paid by foreign corporations that have a U.S. source under section 861(a)(2)(B).

Relation to other articles

Notwithstanding the foregoing limitations on source country taxation of dividends, the saving clause of paragraph 4 of Article 1 permits the United States to tax dividends received by its residents and citizens as if the Convention had not come into effect.

The benefits of this Article are also subject to the provisions of Article 17 (Limitation on Benefits). Thus, if a resident of the other Contracting State is the beneficial owner of dividends paid by a U.S. corporation, the shareholder must qualify for treaty benefits under at least one of the tests of Article 17 in order to receive the benefits of this Article.

ARTICLE 11 (INTEREST)

Article 11 specifies the taxing jurisdiction over interest income of the States of source and residence and defines the terms necessary to apply the article. The Article provides for full residence country taxation of such interest and a limited source country right to tax.

Paragraph 1

Paragraph 1 preserves the residence country's general right to tax its residents on interest arising in the other State. For interest from any other source paid to a resident, Article 22 (Other Income) grants the residence country exclusive taxing jurisdiction (other than for interest attributable to a permanent establishment or fixed base in the other State).

Paragraph 2

Paragraph 2 allows the State where the interest arises, as defined in paragraph 7, to tax the interest, except as provided in paragraph 3. If, however, the beneficial owner of the interest is a resident of the other Contracting State, the tax may not exceed the maximum rates specified in subparagraphs (a) and (b). The term "beneficial owner" is not defined in the Convention, and is, therefore, defined as under the internal law of the country imposing tax (i.e., the source country). The beneficial owner of the interest for purposes of Article 11 is the person to which the interest income is attributable for tax purposes under the laws of the source State. Thus, if interest arising in a Contracting State is received by a nominee or agent that is a resident of the other State on behalf of a person that is not a resident of that other State, the interest is not entitled to the benefits of this Article. However, a dividend received by a nominee on behalf of a resident of that other State would be entitled to benefits. These limitations are confirmed by paragraph 8 of the OECD Commentaries to Article 11. See also paragraph 24 of the OECD Commentaries to Article 1 (General Scope).

Subparagraph (a) applies to interest beneficially owned by any financial institution (including an insurance company). The rate of tax at source on such interest may not exceed 4.95 percent of the gross amount of the interest. This rate is based on Venezuela's statutory rate of interest withholding when the payment is made to financial institutions.

Subparagraph (b) applies to all other categories of interest that are not dealt with in subparagraph (a) or paragraph 3. That subparagraph imposes a ceiling of 10 percent of the gross amount of such interest.

Paragraph 3

Paragraph 3 specifies three categories of interest that are exempt from source State taxation. The first category, described in subparagraph 3 (a), is interest paid by that State or one of its political subdivisions or local authorities. The second category, described in subparagraph 3 (b), is interest beneficially owned by the other State or one of its political subdivisions, local authorities or by an instrumentality wholly owned by that State. Paragraph 9 of the Protocol defines these instrumentalities to include the U.S. Export-Import Bank, the Federal Reserve Banks, the Overseas Private Investment Corporation, the Venezuelan Banco de Comercio Exterior, the Banco Central de Venezuela and the Fondo de Inversiones de Venezuela. The Protocol also allows the competent authorities to agree on the inclusion of other such instrumentalities. The function of the Banco de Comercio Exterior, according to the legislation creating it, is the "promotion of exports and investments." The legislation creating the Fondo de Inversiones de Venezuela states that the objectives of that entity are "to implement the privatization and restructuring of public entities, to assist in the financing of the development of the economic structure of the country, and the promotion of approved international investment projects." The Banco Central de Venezuela is the Central Bank of Venezuela.

Finally, subparagraph 3 (c) describes the third category of interest which shall be exempt from source State taxation, interest beneficially owned by a resident of the other State with respect to debt obligations that have been made, guaranteed or insured, directly or indirectly, by that other State or one of its wholly owned instrumentalities described in the preceding two sentences.

Paragraph 4

Paragraph 4 provides anti-abuse exceptions to the source State reductions in tax provided in paragraphs 2 and 3 for two classes of interest payments.

The first exception, in subparagraph (a) of paragraph 4, deals with so-called "contingent interest." Under this provision interest arising in one of the Contracting States that is determined by reference to the receipts, sales, income, profits or other cash flow of the debtor or a related person, to any change in the value of any property of the debtor or a related person or to any dividend, partnership distribution or similar payment made by the debtor to a related person, also may be taxed in the Contracting State in which it arises, and according to the laws of that State, but if the beneficial owner is a resident of the other Contracting State, the gross amount of the interest may be taxed at a rate not exceeding the rate prescribed in subparagraph b) of paragraph 2 of Article 10 (Dividends).

The second exception, in subparagraph (b) of paragraph 4, is consistent with the policy of Code sections 860E(e) and 860G(b) that excess inclusions with respect to a real estate mortgage investment conduit (REMIC) should bear full U.S. tax in all cases. Without a full tax at source foreign purchasers of residual interests would have a competitive advantage over U.S. purchasers at the time these interests are initially offered. Also, absent this rule the U.S. fisc would suffer a revenue loss with respect to mortgages held in a REMIC because of opportunities for tax avoidance created by differences in the timing of taxable and economic income produced by these interests.

Paragraph 5

The term "interest" as used in Article 11 is defined in paragraph 2 to include, inter alia, income from debt claims of every kind, whether or not secured by a mortgage. Penalty charges for late payment are excluded from the definition of interest. Interest that is paid or accrued subject to a contingency is within the ambit of Article 11. This includes income from a debt obligation carrying the right to participate in profits, unless such income is characterized as a dividend under the laws of the source State. The term does not, however, include amounts that are treated as dividends under Article 10 (Dividends).

The term interest also includes income that is treated as interest by the taxation law of the Contracting State in which the income arises. Thus, for purposes of the Convention amounts that the United States will treat as interest include (i) the difference between the issue price and the stated redemption price at maturity of a debt instrument, i.e., original issue discount (OID), which may be wholly or partially realized on the disposition of a debt instrument (section 1273), (ii) amounts that are imputed interest on a deferred sales contract (section 483), (iii) amounts treated as interest or OID under the stripped bond rules (section 1286), (iv) amounts treated as original issue discount under the below-market interest rate rules (section 7872), (v) a partner's distributive share of a partnership's interest income (section 702), (vi) the interest portion of periodic payments made under a "finance lease" or similar contractual arrangement that in substance is a borrowing by the nominal lessee to finance the acquisition of property, (vii) amounts included in the income of a holder of a residual interest in a REMIC (section 860E), because these amounts generally are subject to the same taxation treatment as interest under U.S. tax law, and (viii) embedded interest with respect to notional principal contracts.

Paragraph 6

Paragraph 6 provides an exception to the taxing rules of paragraphs 2 and 3 in cases where the beneficial owner of the interest carries on business through a permanent establishment in the State of source or performs independent personal services from a fixed base situated in that State and the interest is attributable to that permanent establishment or fixed base. In such cases the provisions of Article 7 (Business Profits) or Article 14 (Independent Personal Services) will apply and the State of source will retain the right to impose tax on such interest income on a net basis.

In the case of a permanent establishment or fixed base that once existed in the State but that no longer exists, the provisions of paragraph 6 also apply, by virtue of paragraph 8 of Article 7 (Business Profits), to interest that would be attributable to such a permanent establishment or fixed base if it did exist in the year of payment or accrual. See the Technical Explanation of paragraph 8 of Article 7.

Paragraph 7

Paragraph 7 provides a general source rule with two exceptions. Interest is considered to arise in a Contracting State if paid by a resident of that State (including that State itself or one of its political subdivisions or local authorities). As a first exception, interest that is borne by a permanent establishment or fixed base in one of the States is considered to arise in that State. For this purpose, interest is considered to be borne by a permanent establishment or fixed base if it is allocable to taxable income of that permanent establishment or fixed base. Likewise, if the person paying the interest, whether or not he is a resident of a Contracting State, derives profits that are taxable in one of the Contracting States on a net basis under paragraphs of Article 5 (Income from Immovable Property (Real Property)) or paragraph 1 of Article 13 (Gains), and the interest is allocable to those profits, it shall be deemed to arise in that State.

Paragraph 8

Paragraph 8 provides that in cases involving special relationships between persons, Article 11 applies only to that portion of the total interest payments that would have been made absent such special relationships (i.e., an arm's-length interest payment). Any excess amount of interest paid remains taxable according to the laws of the United States and Venezuela, respectively, with due regard to the other provisions of the Convention. Thus, if the excess amount would be treated under the source country's law as a distribution of profits by a corporation, such amount could be taxed as a dividend rather than as interest, but the tax would be subject, if appropriate, to the rate limitations of paragraph 2 of Article 10 (Dividends).

The term "special relationship" is not defined in the Convention. In applying this paragraph the United States considers the term to include the relationships described in Article 9, which in turn correspond to the definition of "control" for purposes of section 482 of the Code.

This paragraph does not address cases where, owing to a special relationship between the payer and the beneficial owner or between both of them and some other person, the amount of the interest is less than an arm's-length amount. In those cases a transaction may be characterized to reflect its substance and interest may be imputed consistent with the definition of interest in paragraph 2. Consistent with Article 9 (Associated Enterprises) the United States would apply section 482 or 7872 of the Code to determine the amount of imputed interest in those cases.

Relation to other articles

Notwithstanding the foregoing limitations on source country taxation of interest, the saving clause of paragraph 4 of Article 1 permits the United States to tax its residents and citizens as if the Convention had not come into force.

As with other benefits of the Convention, the benefits of limited source State taxation under paragraphs 2, 3 and 4 (a), are available to a resident of the other State only if that resident is entitled to those benefits under the provisions of Article 17 (Limitation on Benefits).

ARTICLE 11A (BRANCH TAX)

Article 11A permits the United States to impose its branch taxes on the "dividend equivalent amount" and the "excess interest" of a Venezuelan company that derives business profits attributable to a U.S. permanent establishment or which derives income subject to tax on a net basis in the United States under Articles 6 (Income from Immovable Property (Real Property) or 13 (Gains). These branch taxes are imposed under Code section 884. The tax on the dividend equivalent amount is limited to 5 percent, the same rate that applies to direct investment dividends. The tax on excess interest is limited to 10 percent, except in the case of persons referred to in subparagraph (a) of paragraph 11 (Interest), in which case the tax is limited to 4.95 percent.

More specifically, with respect to profit, Article 11A permits the United States generally to impose its branch profits tax on a corporation resident Venezuela to the extent of the corporation's (i) business profits that are attributable to a permanent establishment in the United States (ii) income that is subject to taxation on a net basis because the corporation has elected under section 882(d) of the Code to treat income from real property not otherwise taxed on a net basis as effectively connected income and (iii) gain from the disposition of a United States real property interest, other than an interest in a United States real property holding corporation. The United States may not impose its branch profits tax on the business profits of a corporation resident in Venezuela that are effectively connected with a U.S. trade or business but that are not attributable to a permanent establishment and are not otherwise subject to U.S. taxation under Article 6 or paragraph 1 of Article 13.

Paragraph 10 (a) of the Protocol specifies that the term "dividend equivalent amount" used in subparagraph (a) shall have the meaning it has under section 884 of the Code, as amended from time to time, provided the amendments are consistent with the purpose of the branch profits tax. Generally, the dividend equivalent amount for a particular year is the income described above that is included in the corporation's effectively connected earnings and profits for that year, after payment of the corporate tax under Articles 6, 7 or 13, reduced for any increase in the branch's U.S. net equity during the year or increased for any reduction in its U.S. net equity during the year. U.S. net equity is U.S. assets less U.S. liabilities. See, Treas. Reg. section 1.884-1. The dividend equivalent amount for any year approximates the dividend that a U.S. branch office would have paid during the year if the branch had been operated as a separate U.S. subsidiary company.

With respect to interest, Article 11A permits the United States generally to impose its branch profits tax on a corporation resident Venezuela to the extent of the corporation's "excess interest," which is defined in paragraph 10(b) of the Protocol. In general, excess interest is the portion of the entire enterprise's interest expense that is allocated to the branch over the amount of interest paid by the U.S. branch, and a tax is applied to the amount of that deemed payment. Such excess interest is deemed to arise in Contracting State in which that branch is located. The rate of tax on the deemed payment is limited to 10 percent, the rate generally applicable to interest payments to residents of the other Contracting State. However, in the case of interest deemed paid by the branch of a financial institution, the rate of tax is limited to 4.95 percent, the rate generally applicable to interest beneficially owned by financial institutions. The formula for calculating excess interest does not require that interest be fully deductible in one year. Rather, interest may be "excess interest" even though not deductible in a particular year if it is allocable to the U.S. income under U.S. domestic law rules.

Just as under Venezuela's current system there is no shareholder level tax on dividends, there is also no Venezuelan tax on the dividend equivalent amount of branch profits or on excess interest. Nevertheless, this Article is drafted reciprocally, and thus, if in the future Venezuela should adopt branch taxes, it may apply them to U.S. companies, subject to the limitations of this Article.

ARTICLE 12 (ROYALTIES)

Article 12 specifies the taxing jurisdiction over royalties of the States of residence and source, and defines the terms necessary to apply the article.

Paragraph 1

Paragraph 1 provides that a royalty derived by a resident of a Contracting State that arises in the other Contracting State may be taxed in the first-mentioned Contracting States. For royalties from any other source paid to a resident, Article 22 (Other Income) grants the residence country exclusive taxing jurisdiction (other than for royalties attributable to a permanent establishment or fixed base in the other State).

Paragraphs 2 and 3

Paragraph 2 allows the State where the royalty arises, as defined in paragraph 5, to tax the royalty. If, however, the beneficial owner of the royalty is a resident of the other Contracting State, the tax may not exceed the maximum rates specified in subparagraphs 2(a) and 2(b) for the corresponding classes of royalties described in paragraph 3. The term "beneficial owner" is not defined in the Convention, and is, therefore, defined as under the internal law of the country imposing tax (i.e., the source country). The beneficial owner of the royalty for purposes of Article 12 is the person to which the royalty income is attributable for tax purposes under the laws of the source State. Thus, if a royalty arising in a Contracting State is received by a nominee or agent that is a resident of the other State on behalf of a person that is not a resident of that other State, the royalty is not entitled to the benefits of this Article. However, a royalty received by a nominee on behalf of a resident of that other State would be entitled to benefits. These limitations are confirmed by paragraph 4 of the OECD Commentaries to Article 12. See also paragraph 24 of the OECD Commentaries to Article 1.

Subparagraph (a) of paragraph 2 limits the tax at source to 5 percent of the gross amount of royalties described in subparagraph (a) of paragraph 3. These are royalties for the use of, or the right to use, industrial, commercial or scientific equipment. The U.S. Model and most U.S. treaties treat such income as business profits, and not as royalties. The Convention includes this income within the scope of Article 12, but applies a rate lower than that applied to industrial royalties. Rental payments for ships, aircraft and containers used in international traffic are, however, taxed under Article 8 (Shipping and Air Transport), not Article 12.

Subparagraph (b) of paragraph 2 limits the tax at source to 10 percent of the gross amount of royalties described in subparagraph (b) of paragraph 3. The royalties that fall into this category are payments for the use of, or the right to use, any copyright or literary, dramatic, musical, artistic, or scientific work, including cinematographic films, tapes, and other means of image or sound reproduction, any patent, trademark, design or model, plan, secret formula or process, or other like right or property, or for information concerning industrial, commercial or scientific experience. Gains derived from the alienation of such right or property, to the extent that such gains are contingent on their productivity, use, or disposition, are also included within this class of royalties. Subparagraph (b) of paragraph 2 limits the tax at source on such royalties to 10 percent of the gross amount of the royalty.

The term "royalties" is defined in the Convention and therefore is generally independent of domestic law. Thus, the United States would impose a 5 percent tax on payments for the rental of drilling rigs, even though such payments would not be characterized as royalties under domestic law. Certain terms used in the definition are not defined in the Convention, but these may be defined under domestic tax law. For example, the term "secret process or formulas" is found in the Code, and its meaning has been elaborated in the context of sections 351 and 367. See Rev. Rul. 55-17, 1955-1 C.B. 388; Rev. Rul. 64-56, 1964-1 C.B. 133; Rev. Proc. 69-19, 1969-2 C.B. 301.

Consideration for the use or right to use cinematographic films, or works on film, tape, or other means of image or sound reproduction in radio or television broadcasting is specifically included in the definition of royalties. It is intended that subsequent technological advances in the field of radio and television broadcasting will not affect the inclusion of payments relating to the use of such means of reproduction in the definition of royalties.

If an artist who is resident in one Contracting State records a performance in the other Contracting State, retains a copyrighted interest in a recording, and receives payments for the right to use the recording based on the sale or public playing of the recording, then the right of such other Contracting State to tax those payments is governed by Article 12. See Boulez v. Commissioner, 83 T.C. 584 (1984), aff'd, 810 F.2d 209 (D.C. Cir. 1986).

Computer software generally is protected by copyright laws around the world. Under the Convention, consideration received for the use, or the right to use, computer software is treated either as royalties or as business profits, depending on the facts and circumstances of the trans- action giving rise to the payment.

The primary factor in determining whether consideration received for the use, or the right to use, computer software is treated as royalties or as business profits, is the nature of the rights transferred. See, Treas. Reg. section 1.861-18. The fact that the transaction is characterized as a license for copyright law purposes is not dispositive. For example, as was discussed and understood among the negotiators, a typical retail sale of "shrink wrap" software generally will not be considered to give rise to royalty income, even though for copyright law purposes it may be characterized as a license.

The means by which the computer software is transferred are not relevant for purposes of the analysis. Consequently, if software is electronically transferred but the rights obtained by the transferee are substantially equivalent to rights in a program copy, the payment will be considered business profits.

The term "royalties" also includes gain derived from the alienation of any right or property that would give rise to royalties, to the extent the gain is contingent on the productivity, use, or further alienation thereof. Gains that are not so contingent are dealt with under Article 13 (Gains).

The term "industrial, commercial, or scientific experience" (sometimes referred to as "know-how") has the meaning ascribed to it in paragraph 11 of the Commentary to Article 12 of the OECD Model Convention. Consistent with that meaning, the term may include information that is ancillary to a right otherwise giving rise to royalties, such as a patent or secret process.

Know-how also may include, in limited cases, technical information that is conveyed through technical or consultancy services. It does not include general educational training of the user's employees, nor does it include information developed especially for the user, such as a technical plan or design developed according to the user's specifications. Thus, as provided in paragraph 11 of the Commentaries to Article 12 of the OECD Model, the term "royalties" does not include payments received as consideration for after-sales service, for services rendered by a seller to a purchaser under a guarantee, or for pure technical assistance.

The term "royalties" also does not include payments for professional services (such as architectural, engineering, legal, managerial, medical, software development services). For example, income from the design of a refinery by an engineer (even if the engineer employed know-how in the process of rendering the design) or the production of a legal brief by a lawyer is not income from the transfer of know-how taxable under Article 12. As provided in paragraph 11 of the Protocol, payments received as consideration for technical services or assistance (including studies or surveys of a scientific, geological or technical nature), for engineering works (including the plans related thereto), or for consultancy or supervisory services or assistance shall be considered payments to which the provisions of Article 7 (Business Profits) or Article 14 (Independent Personal Services) apply. Professional services may be embodied in property that gives rise to royalties, however. Thus, if a professional contracts to develop patentable property and retains rights in the resulting property under the development contract, subsequent license payments made for those rights would be royalties.

Paragraph 4

This paragraph provides an exception to the rule of paragraph 2 that gives the state of source limited gross-basis taxing jurisdiction in cases where the beneficial owner of the royalties carries on business through a permanent establishment in the state of source or performs independent personal services from a fixed base situated in that state and the royalties are attributable to that permanent establishment or fixed base. In such cases the provisions of Article 7 (Business Profits) or Article 14 (Independent Personal Services) will apply.

The provisions of paragraph 8 of Article 7 (Business Profits) apply to this paragraph. For example, royalty income that is attributable to a permanent establishment or a fixed base and that accrues during the existence of the permanent establishment or fixed base, but is received after the permanent establishment or fixed base no longer exists, remains taxable under the provisions of Articles 7 (Business Profits) or 14 (Independent Personal Services), respectively, and not under this Article.

Paragraph 5

Paragraph 5 provides a source rule for royalties. Under this provision, royalties shall be deemed to arise in a Contracting State when they are in consideration for the use of, or the right to use, property, information or experience in that State. This source rule is in general accord with the "place-of-use" test of section 861(a)(4) of the Code.

Paragraph 6

Paragraph 6 provides that in cases involving special relationships between the payor and beneficial owner of royalties, Article 12 applies only to the extent the royalties would have been paid absent such special relationships (i.e., an arm's-length royalty). Any excess amount of royalties paid remains taxable according to the laws of the two Contracting States with due regard to the other provisions of the Convention. If, for example, the excess amount is treated as a distribution of corporate profits under domestic law, such excess amount will be taxed as a dividend rather than as royalties, but the tax imposed on the dividend payment will be subject to the rate limitations of paragraph 2 of Article 10 (Dividends).

Relation to other articles

Notwithstanding the foregoing limitations on source country taxation of royalties, the saving clause of paragraph 4 of Article 1 (General Scope) permits the United States to tax its residents and citizens as if the Convention had not come into force.

As with other benefits of the Convention, the benefits of exclusive residence State taxation of royalties under paragraph 1 of Article 12 are available to a resident of the other State only if that resident is entitled to those benefits under Article 17 (Limitation on Benefits).

ARTICLE 13 (GAINS)

Article 13 assigns either primary or exclusive taxing jurisdiction over gains or income from the alienation of property to the State of residence or the State of source and defines the terms necessary to apply the Article.

Paragraph 1

Paragraph 1 of Article 13 preserves the non-exclusive right of the State of source to tax gains from the alienation of real property situated in that State. The paragraph therefore permits the United States to apply section 897 of the Code to tax gains derived by a resident of the other Contracting State that are attributable to the alienation of real property situated in the United States (as defined in paragraph 2). Gains attributable to the alienation of real property include gain from any other property that is treated as a real property interest within the meaning of paragraph 2.

Paragraph 2

This paragraph defines the term "real property situated in the other Contracting State." The term includes real property referred to in Article 6 (i.e., an interest in the real property itself) an interest in a partnership, trust or estate to the extent that its assets consist of real property situated in that other State, a "United States real property interest" (when the United States is the other Contracting State under paragraph 1), and an equivalent interest in real property situated in Venezuela. The OECD Model does not refer to real property interests other than the real property itself, and the United States has entered a reservation on this point with respect to the OECD Model, reserving the right to apply its tax under FIRPTA to all real estate gains encompassed by that provision.

Under section 897(c) of the Code the term "United States real property interest" includes shares in a U.S. corporation that owns sufficient U.S. real property interests to satisfy an asset-ratio test on certain testing dates. The term also includes certain foreign corporations that have elected to be treated as U.S. corporations for this purpose. Section 897(i). In applying paragraph 1 the United States will look through distributions made by a REIT. Accordingly, distributions made by a REIT are taxable under paragraph 1 of Article 13 (not under Article 10 (Dividends)) when they are attributable to gains derived from the alienation of real property.

Paragraph 3

Paragraph 3 of Article 13 deals with the taxation of certain gains from the alienation of movable property forming part of the business property of a permanent establishment that an enterprise of a Contracting State has in the other Contracting State or of movable property pertaining to a fixed base available to a resident of a Contracting State in the other Contracting State for the purpose of performing independent personal services. This also includes gains from the alienation of such a permanent establishment (alone or with the whole enterprise) or of such fixed base. Such gains may be taxed in the State in which the permanent establishment or fixed base is located.

A resident of the other Contracting State that is a partner in a partnership doing business in the United States generally will have a permanent establishment in the United States as a result of the activities of the partnership, assuming that the activities of the partnership rise to the level of a permanent establishment. Rev. Rul. 91-32, 1991-1 C.B. 107. Further, under paragraph 3, the United States generally may tax a partner's distributive share of income realized by a partnership on the disposition of movable property forming part of the business property of the partnership in the United States.

Paragraph 8 of Article 7 (Business Profits) refers to paragraph 3 of Article 13. That rule clarifies that income that is attributable to a permanent establishment or a fixed base, but that is deferred and received after the permanent establishment or fixed base no longer exists, may nevertheless be taxed by the State in which the permanent establishment or fixed base was located. Thus, under Article 13, gains derived by a resident of a Contracting State from the sale of movable property forming part of the business property of a permanent establishment in the other Contracting State may be taxed by that other State even if the income is deferred and received after the permanent establishment no longer exists.

Paragraph 4

This paragraph limits the taxing jurisdiction of the state of source with respect to gains from the alienation of ships, aircraft, or containers operated in international traffic or movable property pertaining to the operation of such ships, aircraft, or containers. Under paragraph 4 when such income is derived by an enterprise of a Contracting State it is taxable only in that Contracting State. Notwithstanding paragraph 3, the rules of this paragraph apply even if the income is attributable to a permanent establishment maintained by the enterprise in the other Contracting State. This result is consistent with the general rule under Article 8 (Shipping and Air Transport) that confers exclusive taxing rights over international shipping and air transport income on the state of residence of the enterprise deriving such income.

Paragraph 5

Paragraph 5 grants to the State of residence of the alienator the exclusive right to tax gains from the alienation of property other than property referred to in paragraphs 1 through 4. For example, gain derived from shares, other than shares described in paragraphs 2 or 3, debt instruments and various financial instruments, may be taxed only in the State of residence, to the extent such income is not otherwise characterized as income taxable under another article (e.g., Article 10 (Dividends) or Article 11 (Interest)). Similarly, gain derived from the alienation of tangible personal property, other than tangible personal property described in paragraph 3, may be taxed only in the State of residence of the alienator. Gain derived from the alienation of any property, such as a patent or copyright, that produces income taxable under Article 12 (Royalties) is taxable under Article 12 and not under this article, provided that such gain is of the type described in paragraph 2(b) of Article 12 (i.e., it is contingent on the productivity, use, or disposition of the property). Sales by a resident of a Contracting State of real property located in a third state are not taxable in the other Contracting State, even if the sale is attributable to a permanent establishment located in the other Contracting State.

Relation to other articles

Notwithstanding the foregoing limitations on taxation of certain gains by the State of source, the saving clause of paragraph 4 of Article 1 (General Scope) permits the United States to tax its citizens and residents as if the Convention had not come into effect. Thus, any limitation in this Article on the right of the United States to tax gains does not apply to gains of a U.S. citizens or resident. The benefits of this Article are also subject to the provisions of Article 17 (Limitation on Benefits). Thus, only a resident of a Contracting State that satisfies one of the conditions in Article 17 is entitled to the benefits of this Article.

ARTICLE 14 (INDEPENDENT PERSONAL SERVICES)

The Convention deals in separate articles with different classes of income from personal services. Article 14 deals with the general class of income from independent personal services and Article 15 deals with the general class of income from dependent personal services. Articles 16 and 18 through 21 provide exceptions and additions to these general rules for directors' fees (Article 16); performance income of artistes and sportsmen (Article 18); pensions in respect of personal service income, social security benefits, annuities, alimony, and child support payments (Article 19); government service salaries and pensions (Article 20); and certain income of students,trainees, teachers and researchers (Article 21).

Paragraph 1

Paragraph 1 of Article 14 provides the general rule that an individual who is a resident of a Contracting State and who derives income from performing professional services in an independent capacity will be exempt from tax in respect of that income by the other Contracting State. The income may be taxed in the other Contracting State only if the income is attributable to a fixed base that is regularly available to the individual in that other State for the purpose of performing his services.

Paragraph 1 is subject to the provisions of Article 7 (Business Profits) to ensure that in cases when the source state is allowed to tax income from independent personal services, it will do so only on a net basis. Paragraph 12 of the Protocol states that this Article shall be interpreted along the lines of the 1992 OECD Model Convention (which, at the time this Protocol paragraph was drafted, was the most recent version of the OECD Model). This reference to the OECD Model was inserted to make clear that source tax shall be imposed on net income, as if the income were attributable to a permanent establishment and taxable under Article 7. The U.S. Model achieves the same result in its paragraph 2, which specifies that for purposes of paragraph 1, the income that is taxable in the source State shall be determined under the principles of paragraph 3 of Article 7.

Income derived by persons other than individuals or groups of individuals from the performance of independent personal services is not covered by Article 14. Such income generally would be business profits taxable in accordance with Articles 5 (Permanent Establishment) and 7 (Business Profits). Income derived by employees of such persons generally would be taxable in accordance with Article 15 (Dependent Personal Services).

The term "fixed base" is not defined in the Convention, but its meaning is understood to be similar, but not identical, to that of the term "permanent establishment," as defined in Article 5 (Permanent Establishment). The term "regularly available" also is not defined in the Convention. Whether a fixed base is regularly available to a person will be determined based on all the facts and circumstances. In general, the term encompasses situations where a fixed base is at the disposal of the individual whenever he performs services in that State. It is not necessary that the individual regularly use the fixed base, only that the fixed base be regularly available to him. For example, a U.S. resident partner in a law firm that has offices in the other Contracting State would be considered to have a fixed base regularly available to him in the other State if work space in those offices (whether or not the same space) were made available to him whenever he wished to conduct business in the other State, regardless of how frequently he conducted business in the other State. On the other hand, an individual who had no office in the other State and occasionally rented a hotel room to serve as a temporary office would not be considered to have a fixed base regularly available to him.

It is not necessary that the individual actually use the fixed base. It is only necessary that the fixed base be regularly available to him. For example, if an individual has an office in the other State that he can use if he chooses when he is present in the other State, that fixed base will be considered to be regularly available to him regardless of whether he conducts his activities there.

This Article applies to income derived by a partner resident in the Contracting State that is attributable to personal services of an independent character performed in the other State through a partnership that has a fixed base in that other Contracting State. Income which may be taxed under this Article includes all income attributable to the fixed base in respect of the performance of the personal services carried on by the partnership (whether by the partner himself, other partners in the partnership, or by employees assisting the partners) and any income from activities ancillary to the performance of those services (for example, charges for facsimile services). Income that is not derived from the performance of personal services and that is not ancillary thereto (for example, rental income from subletting office space), will be governed by other Articles of the Convention.

The application of Article 14 to a service partnership may be illustrated by the following example: a partnership formed in the Contracting State has five partners (who agree to split profits equally), four of whom are resident and perform personal services only in the Contracting State at Office A, and one of whom performs personal services from Office B, a fixed base in the other State. In this case, the four partners of the partnership resident in the Contracting State may be taxed in the other State in respect of their share of the income attributable to the fixed base, Office B. The services giving rise to income which may be attributed to the fixed base would include not only the services performed by the one resident partner, but also, for example, if one of the four other partners came to the other State and worked on an Office B matter there, the income in respect of those services also. As noted above, this would be the case regardless of whether the partner from the Contracting State actually visited or used Office B when performing services in the other State.

Paragraph 8 of Article 7 (Business Profits) refers to Article 14. That rule clarifies that income that is attributable to a permanent establishment or a fixed base, but that is deferred and received after the permanent establishment or fixed base no longer exists, may nevertheless be taxed by the State in which the permanent establishment or fixed base was located. Thus, under Article 14, income derived by an individual resident of a Contracting State from services performed in the other Contracting State and attributable to a fixed base there may be taxed by that other State even if the income is deferred and received after there is no longer a fixed base available to the resident in that other State.

Paragraph 2

Paragraph 2 provides a non-exhaustive list of examples of the types of services that are included within the term "professional services of an independent character." It clearly includes those activities listed in paragraph 2 of Article 14 of the OECD Model, such as independent scientific, literary, artistic, educational or teaching activities, as well as the independent activities of physicians, lawyers, engineers, architects, dentists, and accountants. Beyond these examples, the term includes all personal services performed by an individual for his own account, whether as a sole proprietor or a partner, where he receives the income and bears the risk of loss arising from the services. The taxation of income of an individual from those types of independent services which are covered by Articles 16 and 18 through 21 is governed by the provisions of those articles. For example, taxation of the income of a corporate director would be governed by Article 16 (Directors' Fees) rather than Article 14.

Relation to other articles

If an individual resident of Venezuela who is also a U.S. citizen performs independent personal services in the United States, the United States may, by virtue of the saving clause of paragraph 4 of Article 1 (General Scope) tax his income without regard to the restrictions of this Article

ARTICLE 15 (DEPENDENT PERSONAL SERVICES)

Article 15 apportions taxing jurisdiction over remuneration derived by a resident of a Contracting State as an employee between the States of source and residence.

Paragraph 1

The general rule of Article 15 is contained in paragraph 1. Remuneration derived by a resident of a Contracting State as an employee may be taxed by the State of residence, and the remuneration also may be taxed by that other Contracting State to the extent derived from employment exercised (i.e., services performed) in the other Contracting State. Paragraph 1 also provides that the more specific rules of Articles 16 (Directors' Fees), 19 (Pensions, Social Security, Annuities, Alimony and Child Support), 20 (Government Service) and 21 (Students, Trainees, Teachers and Researchers) apply in the case of employment income described in one of these articles. Thus, even though the State of source has a right to tax employment income under Article 15, it may not have the right to tax that income under the Convention if the income is not taxable in the State of source under the provisions of another of the Convention.

Consistent with the corresponding provision of the OECD Model, paragraph 1 applies to "salaries, wages and other similar remuneration," whereas the U.S. Model omits the word "similar." The U.S. Model's deletion of "similar" is intended to make it clear that Article 15 applies to any form of compensation for employment, including payments in kind, regardless of whether the remuneration is "similar" to salaries and wages. Accordingly, the Convention's Protocol paragraph 13 clarifies that "similar remuneration" in the context of this paragraph is to be given a broad interpretation, and is to be understood to encompass benefits in kind received in respect of an employment and any other benefits, whether or not considered as salary in the domestic legislation of both Contracting States. Protocol paragraph 13 also provides a non-exhaustive list of examples of compensation that would be considered "similar remuneration". The list includes, but is not limited to, the use of a residence or automobile, health of life insurance coverage and club memberships, provision of meals, food and groceries, child care, reimbursement of medical, pharmaceutical and dental care expenses, provision of work clothing, toys and school supplies, scholarships, reimbursement of training course expenses, mortuary and burial expenses.

Consistently with section 864(c)(6) of the Code, Article 15 also applies regardless of the timing of actual payment for services. Thus, a bonus paid to a resident of a Contracting State with respect to services performed in the other Contracting State with respect to a particular taxable year would be subject to Article 15 for that year even if it was paid after the close of the year. Similarly, an annuity received for services performed in a taxable year would be subject to Article 15 despite the fact that it was paid in subsequent years. In either case, whether such payments were taxable in the State where the employment was exercised would depend on whether the tests of paragraph 2 were satisfied. Consequently, a person who receives the right to a future payment in consideration for services rendered in a Contracting State would be taxable in that State even if the payment is received at a time when the recipient is a resident of the other Contracting State.

Paragraph 2

Paragraph 2 sets forth an exception to the general rule that employment income may be taxed in the State where the employment is exercised. Under paragraph 2, the State where the employment is exercised may not tax the income from the employment if three conditions are satisfied: (a) the individual is present in the other Contracting State for a period or periods not exceeding 183 days in any 12-month period that begins or ends during the taxable year concerned (i.e., the taxable year in which the services are performed); (b) the remuneration is paid by, or on behalf of, an employer who is not a resident of that other Contracting State; and (c) the remuneration is not borne by a permanent establishment or fixed base that the employer has in that other State. In order for the remuneration to be exempt from tax in the source State, all three conditions must be satisfied. This exception is identical to that set forth in the U.S. and OECD Models.

The 183-day period in condition (a) is to be measured using the "days of physical presence" method. Under this method, the days that are counted include any day in which a part of the day is spent in the host country. (Rev. Rul. 56-24, 1956-1 C.B. 851.) Thus, days that are counted include the days of arrival and departure; weekends and holidays on which the employee does not work but is present within the country; vacation days spent in the country before, during or after the employment period, unless the individual's presence before or after the employment can be shown to be independent of his presence there for employment purposes; and time during periods of sickness, training periods, strikes, etc., when the individual is present but not working. If illness prevented the individual from leaving the country in sufficient time to qualify for the benefit, those days will not count. Also, any part of a day spent in the host country while in transit between two points outside the host country is not counted. These rules are consistent with the description of the 183-day period in paragraph 5 of the Commentary to Article 15 in the OECD Model.

Conditions (b) and (c) are intended to ensure that a Contracting State will not be required to allow a deduction to the payor for compensation paid and at the same time to exempt the employee on the amount received. Accordingly, if a foreign person pays the salary of an employee who is employed in the host State, but a host State corporation or permanent establishment reimburses the payor with a payment that can be identified as a reimbursement, neither condition (b) nor (c), as the case may be, will be considered to have been fulfilled.

The reference to remuneration "borne by" a permanent establishment or fixed base is understood to encompass all expenses that economically are incurred and not merely expenses that are currently deductible for tax purposes. Accordingly, the expenses referred to include expenses that are capitalizable as well as those that are currently deductible. Further, salaries paid by residents that are exempt from income taxation may be considered to be borne by a permanent establishment or fixed base notwithstanding the fact that the expenses will be neither deductible nor capitalizable since the payor is exempt from tax.

Paragraph 3

Paragraph 3 contains a special rule applicable to remuneration for services performed by a resident of a Contracting State in respect of employment as a member of the crew of a ship or aircraft, or as other personnel regularly employed to serve aboard a ship or aircraft, in each case if the ship or aircraft is operated in international traffic. Such remuneration may be taxed only in the State of residence of the employee. In addition to the crew, this provision may cover, for example, in the case of a cruise ship, entertainers, lecturers, etc., employed by the shipping company to serve on the ship throughout its voyage. The Convention's term "member of a crew of a ship or aircraft, or as other personnel regularly employed to serve aboard a ship or aircraft" is meant to clarify that a person who exercises his employment as, for example, an insurance salesman while aboard a ship or aircraft is not covered by this paragraph. This paragraph is inapplicable to persons dealt with in Article 14 (Independent Personal Services). The rule of this paragraph is not meant to differ substantively from the U.S. Model rule in Article 15, paragraph 3, regarding employment as a member of the "regular complement" of a ship or aircraft operated in international traffic.

Relation to other articles

If a U.S. citizen who is resident in Venezuela performs services as an employee in the United States and meets the conditions of paragraph 2 for source country exemption, he nevertheless is taxable in the United States by virtue of the saving clause of paragraph 4 of Article 1 (General Scope).

ARTICLE 16 (DIRECTORS' FEES)

This Article provides that a Contracting State may tax the fees and other similar compensation paid by a company that is a resident of that State for services performed in that State by a resident of the other Contracting State in his capacity as a director of the company. This rule is an exception to the more general rules of Article 14 (Independent Personal Services) and Article 15 (Dependent Personal Services), and applies notwithstanding those articles. Thus, for example, in determining whether a director's fee paid to a non-employee director is subject to tax in the country of residence of the corporation, it is not relevant to establish whether the fee is attributable to a fixed base in that State.

Consistent with the corresponding provision of the OECD Model, Article 16 applies to "directors fees and other similar payments," whereas the U.S. Model omits the word "similar." The U.S. Model's deletion of "similar" is intended to make it clear that Article 16 applies to any form of payment for director services, including payments in kind, regardless of whether the compensation is "similar" to a fee. Accordingly, the Convention's Protocol paragraph 13 clarifies that "similar payments" in the context of this Article is to be given a broad interpretation, and is to be understood to encompass benefits in kind received in respect of an employment and any other benefits, whether or not considered as salary in the domestic legislation of both Contracting States. Protocol paragraph 13 also provides a non-exhaustive list of examples of compensation that would be considered "similar payments". The list includes, but is not limited to, the use of a residence or automobile, health of life insurance coverage and club memberships, provision of meals, food and groceries, child care, reimbursement of medical, pharmaceutical and dental care expenses, provision of work clothing, toys and school supplies, scholarships, reimbursement of training course expenses, mortuary and burial expenses.

The analogous OECD and U.S. provisions reach different results in certain cases. Under the OECD Model provision, a resident of one Contracting State who is a director of a corporation that is resident in the other Contracting State is subject to tax in that other State in respect of his directors' fees regardless of where the services are performed. The United States has entered a reservation with respect to the OECD provision. Under Article 16 of the Convention, the State of residence of the corporation may tax nonresident directors with no time or dollar threshold, but only with respect to remuneration for services performed in that State.

This Article is subject to the saving clause of paragraph 4 of Article 1 (General Scope). Thus, if a U.S. citizen who is a resident of the other Contracting State is a director of a U.S. corporation, the United States may tax his full remuneration regardless of where he performs his services.

ARTICLE 17 (LIMITATION ON BENEFITS)

Purpose of Limitation on Benefits Provisions

The United States views an income tax treaty as a vehicle for providing treaty benefits to residents of the two Contracting States. This statement begs the question of who is to be treated as a resident of a Contracting State for the purpose of being granted treaty benefits. The Commentaries to the OECD Model authorize a tax authority to deny benefits, under substance-over-form principles, to a nominee in one State deriving income from the other on behalf of a third-country resident. In addition, although the text of the OECD Model does not contain express anti-abuse provisions, the Commentaries to Article 1 contain an extensive discussion approving the use of such provisions in tax treaties in order to limit the ability of third-country residents to obtain treaty benefits. The United States holds strongly to the view that tax treaties should include provisions that specifically prevent misuse of treaties by residents of third countries. Consequently, all recent U.S. income tax treaties contain comprehensive Limitation on Benefits provisions.

A treaty that provides benefits to any resident of a Contracting State creates possibilities for "treaty shopping": the use, by residents of third countries, of legal entities established in a Contracting State with a principal purpose of obtaining the benefits of a tax treaty between the United States and the other Contracting State. It is important to note that this definition of treaty shopping does not encompass every case in which a third-country resident establishes an entity in a U.S. treaty partner, and that entity enjoys treaty benefits to which the third-country resident would not itself be entitled. If the third-country resident had substantial reasons for establishing the structure that were unrelated to obtaining treaty benefits, the structure would not fall within the definition of treaty shopping set forth above.

Of course, the fundamental problem presented by this approach is that it is based on the taxpayer's intent, which a tax administrator is normally ill-equipped to identify. In order to avoid the necessity of making this subjective determination, Article 17 sets forth a series of objective tests. The assumption underlying each of these tests is that a taxpayer that satisfies the requirements of any of the tests probably has a real business purpose for the structure it has adopted, or has a sufficiently strong nexus to the other Contracting State (e.g., a resident individual) to warrant benefits even in the absence of a business connection, and that this business purpose or connection is sufficient to justify the conclusion that obtaining the benefits of the treaty is not a principal purpose of establishing or maintaining residence.

For instance, the assumption underlying the active trade or business test under paragraph 1 (d) is that a third-country resident that establishes a "substantial" operation in Venezuela and that derives income from a related activity in the United States would not do so primarily to avail itself of the benefits of the treaty; it is presumed in such a case that the investor had a valid business purpose for investing in Venezuela, and that the link between that trade or business and the U.S. activity that generates the treaty-benefitted income manifests a business purpose for placing the U.S. investments in the entity in Venezuela. It is considered unlikely that the investor would incur the expense of establishing a substantial trade or business in Venezuela simply to obtain the benefits of the Convention. A similar rationale underlies other tests in Article 17.

While these tests provide useful surrogates for identifying actual intent, these mechanical tests cannot account for every case in which the taxpayer was not treaty shopping. Accordingly, Article 17 also includes a provision (paragraph 4) authorizing the competent authority of a Contracting State to grant benefits. While an analysis under paragraph 4 may well differ from that under one of the other tests of Article 17, its objective is the same: to identify investors whose residence in the other State can be justified by factors other than a purpose to derive treaty benefits.

Article 17 and the anti-abuse provisions of domestic law complement each other, as Article 17 effectively determines whether an entity has a sufficient nexus to the Contracting State to be treated as a resident for treaty purposes, while domestic anti-abuse provisions (e.g., business purpose, substance-over-form, step transaction or conduit principles) determine whether a particular transaction should be recast in accordance with its substance. Thus, internal law principles of the source State may be applied to identify the beneficial owner of an item of income, and Article 17 then will be applied to the beneficial owner to determine if that person is entitled to the benefits of the Convention with respect to such income.

Structure of the Article

The structure of the Article is as follows: Paragraph 1 states that a person that is a resident of a Contracting State and derives income from the other Contracting State is entitled to the benefits of the Convention only if that person possesses one of a series of listed attributes. Paragraph 2 provides further limitations on *entidades* and *colectividades* otherwise entitled to benefits under paragraph 1. Paragraph 3 provides an exception to paragraph 1 with respect to former-long-term-residents of the United States. Paragraph 4 provides that benefits also may be granted if the competent authority of the State from which benefits are claimed determines that it is appropriate to provide benefits in that case. Paragraph 5 defines the term "recognized securities exchange" as used in paragraph 1(e).

Paragraph 1

Paragraph 1 states that a person that is a resident of a Contracting State and derives income from the other Contracting State is entitled to the benefits of the Convention only if that person possesses one of a series of listed attributes of a resident of a Contracting State. The benefits otherwise accorded to residents under the Convention include all limitations on source-based taxation under Articles 6 through 16 and 18 through 23, the treaty-based relief from double taxation provided by Article 24 (Relief from Double Taxation), and the protection afforded to residents of a Contracting State under Article 25 (Non-Discrimination). Some provisions do not require that a person be a resident in order to enjoy the benefits of those provisions. These include paragraph 1 of Article 25 (Non-Discrimination), Article 26 (Mutual Agreement Procedure), and Article 28 (Diplomatic Agents and Consular Officers). Article 17 accordingly does not limit the availability of the benefits of these provisions.

Paragraph 1 has seven subparagraphs, each of which describes a category of residents that are entitled to all benefits of the Convention.

It is intended that the provisions of paragraph 1 will be self executing. Unlike the provisions of paragraph 4, discussed below, claiming benefits under paragraph 2 does not require advance competent authority ruling or approval. The tax authorities may, of course, on review, determine that the taxpayer has improperly interpreted the paragraph and is not entitled to the benefits claimed.

Individuals -- Subparagraph 1(a)

Subparagraph (a) provides that an individual resident of a Contracting State will be entitled to all treaty benefits provided that the individual would not be considered a resident of another country under the principles of subparagraphs 3 (a) and 3 (b) of Article 4 (Residence). (This provision, modified from the corresponding provision in the U.S. Model, is intended to prevent a third-country resident individual from using Venezuela's broad residency concept (*"domiciliado"*) to treaty-shop into the United States.) If such an individual receives income as a nominee on behalf of a third-country resident, benefits may be denied under the respective articles of the Convention by the requirement that the beneficial owner of the income be a resident of a Contracting State.

Governmental entities -- Subparagraph 1(b)

Subparagraph (b) provides that the Contracting States, their political subdivisions and local authorities, and instrumentalities and companies wholly-owned by the Contracting States or one of their political subdivisions and local authorities, will be entitled to all benefits of the Convention.

Tax exempt organizations and pension funds -- Subparagraph 1 (c)

Subparagraph 1(c) provides that not-for-profit organizations, including pension funds or private foundations, that because of such status generally are exempt from tax in their State of residence, will be entitled to all the benefits of the Convention if more than half of the beneficiaries, members or participants, if any, in such an organization are themselves entitled to the benefits of the Convention.

Active trade or business -- subparagraph 1(d)

Subparagraph 1(d) sets forth a test under which a resident of a Contracting State may receive treaty benefits with respect to certain items of income that are connected to an active trade or business conducted in its State of residence.

This subparagraph sets forth a three-pronged test that must be satisfied in order for a resident of a Contracting State to be entitled to the benefits of the Convention with respect to a particular item of income. First, the resident must be engaged in the active conduct of a trade or business in its State of residence. Second, the income derived from the other State must be derived in connection with, or be incidental to, that trade or business. Third, if there is common ownership of the activities in both States, the trade or business must be substantial in relation to the activity in the other State that generated the item of income. These determinations are made separately for each item of income derived from the other State. It therefore is possible that a person would be entitled to the benefits of the Convention with respect to one item of income but not with respect to another. If a resident of a Contracting State is entitled to treaty benefits with respect to a particular item of income under paragraph 3, the resident is entitled to all benefits of the Convention insofar as they affect the taxation of that item of income in the other State. Set forth below is a discussion of each of the three prongs of the test under paragraph 3.

Active Conduct of Trade or Business Requirement

The term "trade or business" is not defined in the Convention. Pursuant to paragraph 2 of Article 3 (General Definitions), when determining whether a resident of the other State is entitled to the benefits of the Convention under subparagraph 1(d) with respect to income derived from

U.S. sources, the United States will ascribe to this term the meaning that it has under the law of the United States. Accordingly, the United States competent authority will refer to the regulations issued under section 367(a) for the definition of the term "trade or business." In general, therefore, a trade or business will be considered to be a specific unified group of activities that constitute or could constitute an independent economic enterprise carried on for profit. Furthermore, a corporation generally will be considered to carry on a trade or business only if the officers and employees of the corporation conduct substantial managerial and operational activities. See, Code section 367(a)(3) and the regulations thereunder.

Notwithstanding this general definition of trade or business, subparagraph 1(d) provides that the business of making or managing investments will be considered to be a trade or business only when part of banking, insurance or securities activities conducted by a bank, insurance company, or registered securities dealer. Conversely, such activities conducted by a person other than a bank, insurance company or registered securities dealer will not be considered to be the conduct of an active trade or business, nor would they be considered to be the conduct of an active trade or business if conducted by a banking or insurance company or registered securities dealer, but not as part of the company's banking, insurance or dealer business.

Because a headquarters operation is in the business of managing investments, a company that functions solely as a headquarters company will not be considered to be engaged in an active trade or business for purposes of paragraph 1(d).

Derived in Connection With Requirement

Under the second prong of the test of subparagraph 1(d) income is derived in connection with a trade or business if the income-producing activity in the other State is a line of business that forms a part of or is complementary to the trade or business conducted in the State of residence by the income recipient. Although no definition of the terms "forms a part of" or "complementary" is set forth in the Convention, it is intended that a business activity generally will be considered to "form a part of" a business activity conducted in the other State if the two activities involve the design, manufacture or sale of the same products or type of products, or the provision of similar services. In order for two activities to be considered to be "complementary," the activities need not relate to the same types of products or services, but they should be part of the same overall industry and be related in the sense that the success or failure of one activity will tend to result in success or failure for the other. In cases in which more than one trade or business is conducted in the other State and only one of the trades or businesses forms a part of or is complementary to a trade or business conducted in the State of residence, it is necessary to identify the trade or business to which an item of income is attributable. Royalties generally will be considered to be derived in connection with the trade or business to which the underlying intangible property is attributable. Dividends will be deemed to be derived first out of earnings and profits of the treaty-benefitted trade or business, and then out of other earnings and profits. Interest income may be allocated under any reasonable method consistently applied. A method that conforms to U.S. principles for expense allocation will be considered a reasonable method. The following examples illustrate the application of this provision of subparagraph 1(d).

Example 1. USCo is a corporation resident in the United States. USCo is engaged in an active manufacturing business in the United States. USCo owns 100 percent of the shares of FCo, a corporation resident in Venezuela. FCo distributes USCo products in Venezuela. Since the business activities conducted by the two corporations involve the same products, FCo's distribution business is considered to form a part of USCo's manufacturing business within the meaning of subparagraph 1(d).

Example 2. The facts are the same as in Example 1, except that USCo does not manufacture. Rather, USCo operates a large research and development facility in the United States that licenses intellectual property to affiliates worldwide, including FCo. FCo and other USCo affiliates then manufacture and market the USCo-designed products in their respective markets. Since the activities conducted by FCo and USCo involve the same product lines, these activities are considered to form a part of the same trade or business.

Example 3. Americair is a corporation resident in the United States that operates an international airline. FSub is a wholly-owned subsidiary of Americair resident in Venezuela. FSub operates a chain of hotels in Venezuela that are located near airports served by Americair flights. Americair frequently sells tour packages that include air travel to Venezuela and lodging at FSub hotels. Although both companies are engaged in the active conduct of a trade or business, the businesses of operating a chain of hotels and operating an airline are distinct trades or businesses. Therefore FSub's business does not form a part of Americair's business. However, FSub's business is considered to be complementary to Americair's business because they are part of the same overall industry (travel) and the links between their operations tend to make them interdependent.

Example 4. The facts are the same as in Example 3, except that FSub owns an office building in Venezuela instead of a hotel chain. No part of Americair's business is conducted through the office building. FSub's business is not considered to form a part of or to be complementary to Americair's business. They are engaged in distinct trades or businesses in separate industries, and there is no economic dependence between the two operations.

Example 5. USFlower is a corporation resident in the United States. USFlower produces and sells flowers in the United States and other countries. USFlower owns all the shares of ForHolding, a corporation resident in Venezuela. ForHolding is a holding company that is not engaged in a trade or business. ForHolding owns all the shares of three corporations that are resident in Venezuela: ForFlower, ForLawn, and ForFish. ForFlower distributes USFlower flowers under the USFlower trademark in Venezuela. ForLawn markets a line of lawn care products in the other State under the USFlower trademark. In addition to being sold under the same trademark, ForLawn and ForFlower products are sold in the same stores and sales of each company's products tend to generate increased sales of the other's products. ForFish imports fish from the United States and distributes it to fish wholesalers in Venezuela. For purposes of paragraph 1(d), the business of ForFlower forms a part of the business of USFlower, the business of ForLawn is complementary to the business of USFlower, and the business of ForFish is neither part of nor complementary to that of USFlower.

Finally, a resident in one of the States also will be entitled to the benefits of the Convention with respect to income derived from the other State if the income is "incidental" to the trade or business conducted in the recipient's State of residence. Subparagraph 1(d) provides that income derived from a State will be incidental to a trade or business conducted in the other State if the production of such income facilitates the conduct of the trade or business in the other State. An example of incidental income is the temporary investment of working capital derived from a trade or business.

Substantiality

As indicated above, subparagraph 1(d) provides that income that a resident of a State derives from the other State will be entitled to the benefits of the Convention under paragraph 1 only if the income is derived in connection with a trade or business conducted in the recipient's State of residence and that trade or business is "substantial" in relation to the income-producing activity in the other State. Subparagraph 1(d) provides that whether the trade or business of the income recipient is substantial will be determined based on all the facts and circumstances. These circumstances generally would include the relative scale of the activities conducted in the two States and the relative contributions made to the conduct of the trade or businesses in the two States.

Publicly-Traded Corporations -- Subparagraph 1(e)

Subparagraph (e) applies to publicly-traded corporations, and provides that a company will be entitled to all the benefits of the Convention if in the principal class of shares of the company there is substantial and regular trading on a "recognized securities exchange" located in either Contracting State. The term "recognized securities exchange" is defined in paragraph 5.

The term "principal class of shares" is not defined in the Convention, but will be interpreted by the United States, consistently with other recent U.S. tax treaties and the U.S. Model, to mean that class of shares that represents the majority of the voting power and value of the company. In most cases, this class will be the ordinary or common shares of the company. If the company has more than one class of shares, it is necessary as an initial matter to determine whether one of the classes accounts for more than half of the voting power and value of the company. If so, then only those shares are considered for purposes of the regular trading requirement. If no single class of shares accounts for more than half of the company's voting power and value, it is necessary to identify a group of two or more classes of the company's voting power and value, and then to determine whether each class of shares in this group satisfy the regular trading requirement. Although in a particular case involving a company with several classes of shares it is conceivable that more than one group of classes could be identified that account for more than 50% of the shares, it is only necessary for one such group to satisfy the requirements of this subparagraph in order for the company to be entitled to benefits. Benefits would not be denied to the company even if a second, non-qualifying, group of shares with more than half of the company's voting power and value could be identified.

The term "substantial and regular trading" is not defined in the Convention. In accordance with paragraph 2 of Article 3 (General Definitions), this term will be defined by reference to the domestic tax laws of the State from which treaty benefits are sought, generally the source State. In the case of the United States, this term is understood to have the meaning it has under Treas. Reg. § 1.884-5(d)(4)(i)(B), relating to the branch tax provisions of the Code. Under these regulations, a class of shares is considered to be "regularly traded" if two requirements are met: trades in the class of shares are made in more than de minimis quantities on at least 60 days during the taxable year, and the aggregate number of shares in the class traded during the year is at least 10 percent of the average number of shares outstanding during the year. Sections 1.884-5(d)(4)(i)(A), (ii) and (iii) will not be taken into account for purposes of defining the term "regularly traded" under the Convention. Authorized but unissued shares are not considered for purposes of this test.

As described more fully below, the regular trading requirement can be met by trading on any recognized exchange or exchanges located in either State. Trading on one or more recognized securities exchanges may be aggregated for purposes of this requirement. Thus, a U.S. company could satisfy the regularly traded requirement through trading, in whole or in part, on a recognized securities exchange located in the other Contracting State.

Subsidiaries of Publicly-Traded Corporations -- Subparagraph 1(f)

Subparagraph 1(f) applies to subsidiaries of publicly-traded corporations, and provides a test under which certain companies that are directly or indirectly controlled by companies satisfying the publicly-traded test of subparagraph 1(e) may be entitled to the benefits of the Convention. Under this test, a company will be entitled to the benefits of the Convention if 50 percent or more of each class of shares in the company is directly or indirectly owned by five or fewer companies that are described in subparagraph 1(f).

This test differs from that under subparagraph 1(e) in that 50 percent of each class of the company's shares, not merely the class or classes accounting for more than 50 percent of the company's votes and value, must be held by publicly-traded companies described in subparagraph 1(e). Thus, the test under subparagraph 1(f) considers the ownership of every class of shares outstanding, while the test under subparagraph 1(e) only considers those classes that account for a majority of the company's voting power and value.

Subparagraph 1(f) permits indirect ownership. Consequently, the ownership by publicly-traded companies described in subparagraph 1(e) need not be direct. However, any intermediate owners in the chain of ownership must themselves be entitled to benefits under paragraph 1.

Ownership/Base Erosion -- Subparagraph 1(g)

Subparagraph 1(g) provides a two part test, the so-called ownership and base erosion test. This test applies to any form of legal entity that is a resident of a Contracting State. Both prongs of the test must be satisfied for the resident to be entitled to benefits under this subparagraph.

The ownership prong of the test, under clause i), requires that 50 percent or more of each class of beneficial interests in the person (in the case of a corporation, 50 percent or more of each class of its shares) be owned by persons who are themselves entitled to benefits under other tests of paragraph 1 (i.e., subparagraphs (a), (b), (c), (e), or (f)). The ownership may be indirect through other persons themselves entitled to benefits under paragraph 1.

Trusts may be entitled to benefits under this provision if they are treated as residents under Article 4 (Residence) and they otherwise satisfy the requirements of this subparagraph. For purposes of this subparagraph, the beneficial interests in a trust will be considered to be owned by its beneficiaries in proportion to each beneficiary's actuarial interest in the trust. The interest of a remainder beneficiary will be equal to 100 percent less the aggregate percentages held by income beneficiaries. A beneficiary's interest in a trust will not be considered to be owned by a person entitled to benefits under the other provisions of paragraph 1 if it is not possible to determine the beneficiary's actuarial interest. Consequently, if it is not possible to determine the actuarial interest of any beneficiaries in a trust, the ownership test under clause i) cannot be satisfied, unless all beneficiaries are persons entitled to benefits under the other subparagraphs of paragraph 1.

The base erosion prong of the test under subparagraph 1(g) requires that less than 50 percent of the person's gross income for the taxable year be paid or accrued, directly or indirectly, to non-residents of either State, in the form of payments that are deductible for tax purposes in the entity's State of residence. To the extent they are deductible from the taxable base, trust distributions would be considered deductible payments. Depreciation and amortization deductions, which are not "payments," are disregarded for this purpose. The purposed of this provision is to determine whether the income derived from the source State is in fact subject to the tax regime of either State. Consequently, payments to any resident of either State, are not considered base eroding payments for this purpose (to the extent that these recipients do not themselves base erode to non-residents).

The term "gross income" defined in paragraph 6.

Paragraph 2

Paragraph 2 provides that an *entidad* or *colectividad* formed under the laws of Venezuela otherwise entitled to benefits under paragraph 1 will not be entitled to the benefits of this Convention if 50 percent or more of the vote or value of a "disproportionate" class of interests is owned by persons other than citizens of the United States or residents of the United States or Venezuela that meet the requirements of subparagraphs (a), (b), (c), (e), or (f) of paragraph 1. In general, a class of interests is "disproportionate" for these purposes if the interests entitle the owner to a disproportionately higher participation in the earnings that the company generates in the other State through particular assets or activities of the company. Such participation may take any form, including dividends or redemption payment. Such a class of interests would include so-called alphabet stock or tracking stock that entitles the holder to earnings produced by a particular division or subsidiary of the company in the source State. This provision applies if the disproportionate class of interests is issued by the company claiming benefits, or by a company that controls the company claiming benefits. In this context, control does not require majority ownership.

Paragraph 3

Paragraph 3 provides that notwithstanding paragraph 1, a former long-term resident of the United States shall not be entitled to the benefits of the Convention for the 10-year period following the loss of long-term-resident status if such loss had for one of its principal purposes the avoidance of U.S. tax. Under section 877 of the Code, under which certain former U.S. citizens and long-term residents are subject to U.S. tax, an individual shall be presumed as having a principal purpose to avoid U.S. tax if (1) the average annual net income tax of such individual for the period of 5 taxable years ending before the date of the loss of status is greater than $100,000 (indexed for inflation after 1994); or (2) the net worth of such individual as of the date of the loss of status is $500,000 or more (indexed for inflation after 1994). Paragraph 14 of the Protocol provides that "long-term resident" shall mean any individual who is a lawful permanent resident of the United States in 8 or more taxable years during the preceding 15 taxable years. The paragraph further provides that in determining whether the threshold in the preceding sentence is met, there shall not count any year in which the individual is treated as a resident of Venezuela under this Convention, or as a resident of any country other than the United States under the provisions of any other tax treaty of the United States, and, in either case, the individual does not waive the benefits of such treaty applicable to residents of the other country.

Paragraph 4

Paragraph 4 provides that a resident of one of the States that is not otherwise entitled to the benefits of the Convention may be granted benefits under the Convention if the competent authority of the State from which benefits are claimed so determines. This discretionary provision is included in recognition of the fact that, with the increasing scope and diversity of international economic relations, there may be cases where significant participation by third-country residents in an enterprise of a Contracting State is warranted by sound business practice or long-standing business structures and does not necessarily indicate a motive of attempting to derive unintended Convention benefits.

The competent authority of a State will base a determination under this paragraph on whether the establishment, acquisition, or maintenance of the person seeking benefits under the Convention, or the conduct of such person's operations, has or had as one of its principal purposes the obtaining of benefits under the Convention. Thus, persons that establish operations in one of the States with the principal purpose of obtaining the benefits of the Convention ordinarily will not be granted relief under paragraph 4.

The competent authority may determine to grant all benefits of the Convention, or it may determine to grant only certain benefits. For instance, it may determine to grant benefits only with respect to a particular item of income in a manner similar to subparagraph 1(d). Further, the competent authority may set time limits on the duration of any relief granted.

It is assumed that, for purposes of implementing paragraph 4, a taxpayer will not be required to wait until the tax authorities of one of the States have determined that benefits are denied before he will be permitted to seek a determination under this paragraph. In these circumstances, it is also expected that if the competent authority determines that benefits are to be allowed, they will be allowed retroactively to the time of entry into force of the relevant treaty provision or the establishment of the structure in question, whichever is later.

Finally, there may be cases in which a resident of a Contracting State may apply for discretionary relief to the competent authority of his State of residence. For instance, a resident of a State could apply to the competent authority of his State of residence in a case in which he had been denied a treaty-based credit under Article 24 on the grounds that he was not entitled to benefits of the article under Article 17.

Paragraph 5

Paragraph 5 provides that the term "recognized securities exchange" means, in subparagraph (a), the Caracas and Maracaibo Stock Exchanges, the *Bolsa Electrónica*, and any stock exchanges registered with the *Comisión Nacional De Valores*, in accordance with the *Ley de Mercado de Capitales*, and in subparagraph (b) the NASDAQ System owned by the National Association of Securities Dealers, and any stock exchange registered with the Securities and Exchange Commission as a national securities exchange for purposes of the Securities Exchange Act of 1934. Subparagraph (c) provides that the competent authorities may also agree to recognize additional exchanges for the purposes of this Article.

Paragraph 6

Paragraph 6 provides a definition of the term "gross income" as used in the base erosion test of paragraph 1 (g)(ii). For the purposes of that subparagraph, "gross income" means gross receipts. However, for enterprises engaged in manufacturing, or the production of goods, "gross income" means gross receipts less direct costs of labor and materials attributable to such manufacture or production and paid or payable our of such receipts.

ARTICLE 18 (ARTISTES AND SPORTSMEN)

This Article deals with the taxation in a Contracting State of artistes (i.e., performing artists and entertainers) and sportsmen resident in the other Contracting State from the performance of their services as such. The Article applies both to the income of an entertainer or sportsman who performs services on his own behalf and one who performs services on behalf of another person, either as an employee of that person, or pursuant to any other arrangement. The rules of this Article take precedence, in some circumstances, over those of Articles 14 (Independent Personal Services) and 15 (Dependent Personal Services).

This Article applies only with respect to the income of performing artists and sportsmen. Others involved in a performance or athletic event, such as producers, directors, technicians, managers, coaches, etc., remain subject to the provisions of Articles 14 and 15. In addition, except as provided in paragraph 2, income earned by juridical persons is not covered by Article 18.

Paragraph 1

Paragraph 1 describes the circumstances in which a Contracting State may tax the performance income of an entertainer or sportsman who is a resident of the other Contracting State. Under the paragraph, income derived by an individual resident of a Contracting State from activities as an entertainer or sportsman exercised in the other Contracting State may be taxed in that other State if the amount of the gross receipts derived by the performer exceeds $6,000 (or its equivalent in Venezuela bolivares) for the taxable year. The $6,000 includes expenses reimbursed to the individual or borne on his behalf. If the gross receipts exceed $6,000, the full amount, not just the excess, may be taxed in the State of performance.

The OECD Model provides for taxation by the country of performance of the remuneration of entertainers or sportsmen with no dollar or time threshold. The United States introduces the dollar threshold test in its treaties to distinguish between two groups of entertainers and athletes -- those who are paid relatively large sums of money for very short periods of service, and who would, therefore, normally be exempt from host country tax under the standard personal services income rules, and those who earn relatively modest amounts and are, therefore, not easily distinguishable from those who earn other types of personal service income. The United States has entered a reservation to the OECD Model on this point.

Tax may be imposed under paragraph 1 even if the performer would have been exempt from tax under Articles 14 (Independent Personal Services) or 15 (Dependent Personal Services). On the other hand, if the performer would be exempt from host-country tax under Article 18, but would be taxable under either Article 14 or 15, tax may be imposed under either of those Articles. Thus, for example, if a performer derives remuneration from his activities in an independent capacity, and the remuneration is not attributable to a fixed base, he may be taxed by the host State in accordance with Article 18 if his remuneration exceeds $6,000 annually, despite the fact that he generally would be exempt from host State taxation under Article 14. However, a performer who receives less than the $6,000 threshold amount and therefore is not taxable under Article 18, nevertheless may be subject to tax in the host country under Articles 14 or 15 if the tests for host-country taxability under those Articles are met. For example, if an entertainer who is an independent contractor earns $5,000 of income in a State for the calendar year, but the income is attributable to a fixed base regularly available to him in the State of performance, that State may tax his income under Article 14.

Since it frequently is not possible to know until year-end whether the income an entertainer or sportsman derived from performances in a Contracting State will exceed $6,000, nothing in the Convention precludes that Contracting State from withholding tax during the year and refunding after the close of the year if the taxability threshold has not been met.

As explained in paragraph 9 of the OECD Commentaries to Article 17, Article 18 applies to all income connected with a performance by the entertainer, such as appearance fees, award or prize money, and a share of the gate receipts. Income derived from a Contracting State by a performer who is a resident of the other Contracting State from other than actual performance, such as royalties from record sales and payments for product endorsements, is not covered by this Article, but by other articles of the Convention, such as Article 12 (Royalties) or Article 14 (Independent Personal Services). For example, if an entertainer receives royalty income from the sale of live recordings, the royalty income would be subject to limited source country tax under Article 12, even if the performance was conducted in the source country, although he could be fully taxed in the source country with respect to income from the performance itself under this Article if the dollar threshold is exceeded.

In determining whether income falls under Article 17 or another article, the controlling factor will be whether the income in question is predominantly attributable to the performance itself or other activities or property rights. For instance, a fee paid to a performer for endorsement of a performance in which the performer will participate would be considered to be so closely associated with the performance itself that it normally would fall within Article 18. Similarly, a sponsorship fee paid by a business in return for the right to attach its name to the performance would be so closely associated with the performance that it would fall under Article 18 as well. As indicated in paragraph 9 of the Commentaries to Article 17 of the OECD Model, a cancellation fee would not be considered to fall within Article 18 but would be dealt with under Article 7, 14 or 15.

As indicated in paragraph 4 of the Commentaries to Article 17 of the OECD Model, where an individual fulfills a dual role as performer and non-performer (such as a player-coach or an actor-director), but his role in one of the two capacities is negligible, the predominant character of the individual's activities should control the characterization of those activities. In other cases there should be an apportionment between the performance-related compensation and other compensation.

Consistently with Article 15 (Dependent Personal Services), Article 17 also applies regardless of the timing of actual payment for services. Thus, a bonus paid to a resident of a Contracting State with respect to a performance in the other Contracting State with respect to a particular taxable year would be subject to Article 18 for that year even if it was paid after the close of the year.

Paragraph 2

Paragraph 2 is intended to deal with the potential for abuse when a performer's income does not accrue directly to the performer himself, but to another person. Foreign performers frequently perform in the United States as employees of, or under contract with, a company or other person.

The relationship may truly be one of employee and employer, with no abuse of the tax system either intended or realized. On the other hand, the "employer" may, for example, be a company established and owned by the performer, which is merely acting as the nominal income recipient in respect of the remuneration for the performance (a "star company"). The performer may act as an "employee," receive a modest salary, and arrange to receive the remainder of the income from his performance in another form or at a later time. In such case, absent the provisions of paragraph 2, the income arguably could escape host-country tax because the company earns business profits but has no permanent establishment in that country. The performer may largely or entirely escape host-country tax by receiving only a small salary in the year the services are performed, perhaps small enough to place him below the dollar threshold in paragraph 1. The performer might arrange to receive further payments in a later year, when he is not subject to host-country tax, perhaps as deferred salary payments, dividends or liquidating distributions.

Paragraph 2 seeks to prevent this type of abuse while at the same time protecting the taxpayers' rights to the benefits of the Convention when there is a legitimate employee-employer relationship between the performer and the person providing his services. Under paragraph 2, when the income accrues to a person other than the performer, and the performer or related persons participate, directly or indirectly, in the receipts or profits of that other person, the income may be taxed in the Contracting State where the performer's services are exercised, without regard to the provisions of the Convention concerning business profits (Article 7) or independent personal services (Article 14). Thus, even if the "employer" has no permanent establishment or fixed base in the host country, its income may be subject to tax there under the provisions of paragraph 2. Taxation under paragraph 2 is on the person providing the services of the performer. This paragraph does not affect the rules of paragraph 1, which apply to the performer himself. The income taxable by virtue of paragraph 2 is reduced to the extent of salary payments to the performer, which fall under paragraph 1.

For purposes of paragraph 2, income is deemed to accrue to another person (i.e., the person providing the services of the performer) if that other person has control over, or the right to receive, gross income in respect of the services of the performer. Direct or indirect participation in the profits of a person may include, but is not limited to, the accrual or receipt of deferred remuneration, bonuses, fees, dividends, partnership income or other income or distributions.

Paragraph 2 does not apply if it is established that neither the performer nor any persons related to the performer participate directly or indirectly in the receipts or profits of the person providing the services of the performer. Assume, for example, that a circus owned by a U.S. corporation performs in the other Contracting State, and promoters of the performance in the other State pay the circus, which, in turn, pays salaries to the circus performers. The circus is determined to have no permanent establishment in that State. Since the circus performers do not participate in the profits of the circus, but merely receive their salaries out of the circus' gross receipts, the circus is protected by Article 7 and its income is not subject to host-country tax. Whether the salaries of the circus performers are subject to host-country tax under this Article depends on whether they exceed the $6,000 threshold in paragraph 1.

Since pursuant to Article 1 (General Scope) the Convention only applies to persons who are residents of one of the Contracting States, if the star company is not a resident of one of the Contracting States then taxation of the income is not affected by Article 17 or any other provision of the Convention.

This exception from paragraph 2 for non-abusive cases is not found in the OECD Model. The United States has entered a reservation to the OECD Model on this point.

Paragraph 3

Paragraph 3 provides a special exemption at source of the remuneration of entertainers or athletes whose visit is wholly or mainly supported by the public funds of one or both of the Contracting States, or one of their political subdivisions or local authorities. In such a case, the income shall be taxed only in the Contracting State of which the artiste or sportsman is resident. Some other recent U.S. treaties, including the treaties with Germany and France, provide a similar exception.

Relation to other articles

This Article is subject to the provisions of the saving clause of paragraph 4 of Article 1 (General Scope). Thus, if an entertainer or a sportsman who is resident in the other Contracting State is a citizen of the United States, the United States may tax all of his income from performances in the United States without regard to the provisions of this Article. In addition, benefits of this Article are subject to the provisions of Article 17 (Limitation on Benefits).

ARTICLE 19 (PENSIONS, SOCIAL SECURITY, ANNUITIES, AND CHILD SUPPORT)

This Article deals with the taxation of private (i.e., non-government service) pensions and annuities, social security benefits, and child support payments and with the tax treatment of contributions to pension plans.

Unlike most U.S. tax treaties, the Convention contains no rules for alimony. As a result, alimony payments fall under the rules of Article 22 (Other Income), which, in general, allow items of income of a resident of a Contracting State to be taxed in that State and the State in which the income arises.

Paragraph 1

Paragraph 1 provides that distributions from pensions and other similar remuneration beneficially owned by a resident of a Contracting State in consideration of past employment are taxable only in the State of residence of the beneficiary. It is understood that the term "pension distributions and other similar remuneration," includes both periodic and lump sum payments.

The phrase "pension distributions and other similar remuneration" is intended to encompass payments made by private retirement plans and arrangements in consideration of past employment. In the United States, the plans encompassed by paragraph 1 include: qualified plans under section 401(a), individual retirement plans (including individual retirement plans that are part of a simplified employee pension plan that satisfies section 408(k), individual retirement accounts, individual retirement annuities, section 408(p) accounts, and Roth IRAs under section 408A), non-discriminatory section 457 plans, section 403(a) qualified annuity plans, and section 403(b) plans. The competent authorities may agree that distributions from other plans that generally meet similar criteria to those applicable to other plans established under their respective laws also qualify for the benefits of Paragraph 1. In the United States, these criteria are as follows:

a) The plan must be written;

b) In the case of an employer-maintained plan, the plan must be nondiscriminatory insofar as it (alone or in combination with other comparable plans) must cover a wide range of employees. including rank and file employees, and actually provide significant benefits for the entire range of covered employees;

c) In the case of an employer-maintained plan the plan must contain provisions that severely limit the employees' ability to use plan assets for purposes other than retirement, and in all cases be subject to tax provisions that discourage participants from using the assets for purposes other than retirement; and

d) The plan must provide for payment of a reasonable level of benefits at death, a stated age, or an event related to work status, and otherwise require minimum distributions under rules designed to ensure that any death benefits provided to the participants' survivors are merely incidental to the retirement benefits provided to the participants.

In addition, certain distribution requirements must be met before distributions from these plans would fall under paragraph 1. To qualify as a pension distribution or similar remuneration from a U.S. plan the employee must have been either employed by the same employer for five years or be at least 62 years old at the time of the distribution. In addition, the distribution must be made either (A) on account of death or disability, (B) as part of a series of substantially equal payments over the employee's life expectancy (or over the joint life expectancy of the employee and a beneficiary), or (C) after the employee attained the age of 55. Finally, the distribution must be made either after separation from service or on or after attainment of age 65. A distribution from a pension plan solely due to termination of the pension plan is not a distribution falling under paragraph 1.

Pensions in respect of government service are not covered by this paragraph, but are covered either by paragraph 2 of this Article, if they are in the form of social security benefits, or by paragraph 2 of Article 20 (Government Service). Thus, Article 19 covers section 457, 401(a) and 403(b) plans established for government employees. If a pension in respect of government service is not covered by Article 20 solely because the service is not "in the discharge of functions of a governmental nature," the pension is covered by this Article 19. In the case of Venezuela, in general, pensions in respect of government service will be covered by this article and not by paragraph 2 of Article 20, because, in general, such pensions are not paid by, or out of the funds created by, Venezuela.

Paragraph 2

The treatment of social security benefits is dealt with in paragraph 2. This paragraph provides that payments made by one of the Contracting States under the provisions of its social security or similar legislation to a resident of the other Contracting State or to a citizen of the United States will be taxable in the Contracting State making the payment. This paragraph applies to social security beneficiaries whether they have contributed to the system as private sector or Government employees.

The phrase "similar legislation" is intended to refer to United States tier 1 Railroad Retirement benefits, as is clarified in paragraph 15 of the Protocol.

Paragraph 3

Under paragraph 3, annuities, other than those covered in paragraph 1, that are derived from a Contracting State and that are beneficially owned by an individual resident of the other Contracting State are taxable only in the State from which they are derived. An annuity, as the term is used in this paragraph, means a stated sum paid periodically at stated times during a specific time period, under an obligation to make the payment in return for adequate and full consideration (other than services rendered). An annuity otherwise covered in this paragraph received in consideration for services rendered would be treated as deferred compensation and generally taxable in accordance with Articles 14 (Independent Personal Services) and 15 (Dependent Personal Services).

Paragraph 4

Paragraph 4 deals with child support payments, defined as periodic payments for the support of a minor child made pursuant to a written separation agreement or a decree of divorce, separate maintenance, or compulsory support. Under paragraph 4, such payments made by a resident of a Contracting State to a resident of the other Contracting State are taxable only in that other State.

Relation to other articles

Article 19 is subject to the saving clause of paragraph 4 of Article 1 (General Scope). Thus, for example, a U.S. citizen who is resident of Venezuela and receives a pension payment from the United States may be subject to U.S. tax on the payment, notwithstanding the rules in Article 19 that give Venezuela the exclusive taxing right. Because paragraph 2 does not restrict either State's right to tax social security payments, the saving clause is irrelevant.

ARTICLE 20 (GOVERNMENT SERVICE)

Paragraph 1

Subparagraphs (a) and (b) of paragraph 1 deal with the taxation of government compensation (other than a pension addressed in paragraph 2). Subparagraph (a) provides that remuneration paid by a Contracting State or its political subdivisions or local authorities to any individual who is rendering services to that State, political subdivision or local authority, is exempt from tax by the other State. Under subparagraph (b), such payments are, however, taxable exclusively in the other State (i.e., the host State) if the services are rendered in that other State and the individual is a resident of that State who is either a national of that State or a person who did not become resident of that State solely for purposes of rendering the services. Unlike the OECD Model, the paragraph applies both to government employees and to independent contractors engaged by governments to perform services for them.

Paragraph 2

Paragraph 2 provides rules for the taxation of pensions paid from public funds in respect of governmental services. The paragraph provides that such pensions may be taxed only by the paying State unless the individual recipient is a resident and national of the other State, in which case only the other (residence) State may tax the pension. This rule is subject to the provisions of paragraph 2 of Article 19 (Pensions, Social Security, Annuities, and Child Support), which provides that social security benefits paid by a Contracting State to a resident of the other Contracting State or a citizen of the United States may be taxed by the paying State.

Paragraph 3

The exemptions provided in this Article are limited to remuneration and pensions in respect of services of a governmental nature. Paragraph 3 provides that remuneration and pensions for services to a government-owned business are taxable under the provisions of Articles 14 (Independent Personal Services), 15 (Dependent Personal Services), 16 (Directors' Fees), 18 (Artistes and Athletes), or 19 (Pensions, Social Security, Annuities, and Child Support), as the case may be. Thus, if a local government runs a business, even though the employees who are working for the business are employees of the local government, the compensation of those employees is covered by Article 15 and not Article 20, because the employees are not engaging in a governmental function when they perform their employment duties. Further, the remuneration of artistes or sportsmen who are performing in one Contracting State and are sponsored by the government of the other Contracting State is taxable under paragraph 3 of Article 18 (Artistes and Sportsmen) only in the State sponsoring the performance. Such remuneration is not taxable under this Article because such performers are not employees of the government nor are they discharging functions of a governmental nature. Whether functions are of a governmental nature is determined by reference to the concept of a governmental function in the State in which the income arises.

Relation to other articles

Under paragraph 5(b) of Article 1 (General Scope), the saving clause (paragraph 4 of Article 1) does not apply to the benefits conferred by one of the States under Article 19 if the recipient of the benefits is neither a citizen of that State, nor a person who has been admitted for permanent residence there (i.e., in the United States, a "green card" holder). Thus, a resident of a Contracting State who in the course of performing functions of a governmental nature becomes a resident of the other State (but not a permanent resident), would be entitled to the benefits of this Article.

ARTICLE 21 (STUDENTS, TRAINEES, TEACHERS AND RESEARCHERS)

Paragraph 1

Paragraph 1 of Article 21 provides that a resident of a Contracting State who visits the other Contracting State for the primary purpose of studying at a university or other recognized educational institution, securing training in a professional speciality, or engaging in research of an educational nature shall be exempt from taxation in that Contracting State with respect to certain items of income during such period of study, research, or training. Paragraph 1(b) defines those exempt items of income as 1) payments from abroad, other than compensation for personal services, for maintenance, education, study, research, or training; 2) grants, allowances, or awards from a governmental, religious, charitable, scientific, literary, or educational institution funding the research or studies; and 3) income from personal services performed in that other Contracting State not in excess of $5,000 (or the equivalent in Venezuelan bolivares) per taxable year. The exemptions provided in paragraph 1 are available to the visiting student or trainee for a period not exceeding five years from the beginning of the visit and for such additional period of time as is necessary to complete, as a full-time student, the educational requirements as a candidate for a post-graduate or professional degree from a recognized educational institution.

Paragraph 2

The second paragraph of the Article provides an exemption for residents of a Contracting State who are employed by, or under contract with, a resident of the same Contracting State and who temporarily visit the other Contracting State for the purpose of studying at a university or other recognized educational institution or acquiring technical, professional, or business training or experience in that other Contracting State, provided such training is from a person other than the employer or contractor. Such student or trainee is exempt from taxation in the other Contracting State for a period of twelve months on personal services income not in excess of $8,000 (or the equivalent in Venezuelan bolivares) during that period.

The monetary limits provided in paragraphs 1 and 2 are in addition to, and not in lieu of, other exemptions provided by the Code. Thus, an unmarried resident of Venezuela who is temporarily present in the United States for the primary purpose of studying at a university would be entitled to exclude $5,000 of income from the performance of personal services and, in addition, would be entitled to the personal exemption allowed by section 151 of the Code, as provided by section 873 (b) of the Code.

Paragraph 3

Paragraph 3 provides a limited exemption from tax in a Contracting State for income from personal services of individuals resident in the other Contracting State, who are temporarily present in the first-mentioned State for the purpose of teaching or carrying on research at a recognized educational or research institution in that first State. Unlike the exemptions in paragraphs 1 and 2, no dollar limit to these benefits for teachers and researchers is specified. However, paragraph 3 establishes that the host country exemption provided shall only last for two years from the date of entry of that individual in the host State, and in no case shall the benefits of the paragraph be granted for more than five taxable years to any individual.

Paragraph 4

Paragraph 4 establishes that the exemptions provided in this Article do not apply to income from research if such research is undertaken primarily for the private benefit of a specific person or persons. For example, personal service income arising from research at a corporate research facility would, in general, not qualify as exempt income.

Relation to other articles

The benefits conferred by the other Contracting State under Article 20 are subject to the provisions of the saving clause in paragraph 4 of Article 1 (General Scope) as modified by paragraph 5(b) of Article 1. With respect to the United States, the modified saving clause applies to U.S. citizens and persons having immigrant status in the United States ("green card" holders). Thus, the provisions of paragraph 1 which would exempt a Venezuelan resident from taxation as a student in the United States are overridden by the saving clause if that student is a U.S. citizen or green card holder. On the other hand, if a student (who is not a citizen or a green card holder) acquires residence in the United States for tax purposes during that period of study or training, he will be exempt from tax in the United States on those certain items of income.

ARTICLE 22 (OTHER INCOME)

Article 22 generally assigns taxing jurisdiction over income not dealt with in the other articles (Articles 6 through 16 and 18 through 21) of the Convention to the State of residence of the beneficial owner of the income and defines the terms necessary to apply the article. However, the other State may also tax such income if it arises in the other State. An item of income is "dealt with" in another article if it is the type of income described in the article and it has its source in a Contracting State. For example, all royalty income that arises in a Contracting State and that is beneficially owned by a resident of the other Contracting State is "dealt with" in Article 12 (Royalties).

Examples of items of income commonly covered by Article 22 include income from gambling, punitive (but not compensatory) damages, covenants not to compete, and income from certain financial instruments to the extent derived by persons not engaged in the trade or business of dealing in such instruments (unless the transaction giving rise to the income is related to a trade or business, in which case it is dealt with under Article 7 (Business Profits)). In this Convention, alimony payments are also covered in Article 22. The article also applies to items of income that are not dealt with in the other articles because of their source or some other characteristic. For example, Article 11 (Interest) addresses only the taxation of interest arising in a Contracting State. Interest arising in a third State that is not attributable to a permanent establishment, therefore, is subject to Article 22.

Distributions from partnerships and distributions from trusts are not generally dealt with under Article 22 because partnership and trust distributions generally do not constitute income. Under the Code, partners include in income their distributive share of partnership income annually, and partnership distributions themselves generally do not give rise to income. Also, under the Code, trust income and distributions have the character of the associated distributable net income and therefore would generally be covered by another article of the Convention. See, Code section 641 et seq.

Paragraph 1

Paragraph 1 provides that items of income not dealt with in other articles that are earned by a resident of a Contracting State generally will be taxable in the State of residence. This right of taxation applies whether or not the residence State exercises its right to tax the income covered by the Article. The residence taxation provided by paragraph 1 applies only when a resident of a Contracting State is the beneficial owner of the income. This is understood from the phrase "income of a resident of a Contracting State." Thus, source taxation of income not dealt with in other articles of the Convention is not limited by paragraph 1 if it is nominally paid to a resident of the other Contracting State, but is beneficially owned by a resident of a third State.

Paragraph 2

Paragraph 2 provides an exception to the general rule of paragraph 1 for income, other than income from real property, that is attributable to a permanent establishment or fixed base maintained in a Contracting State by a resident of the other Contracting State. The taxation of such income is governed by the provisions of Articles 7 (Business Profits) and 14 (Independent Personal Services). Therefore, income arising outside the United States that is attributable to a permanent establishment maintained in the United States by a resident of Venezuela generally would be taxable by the United States under the provisions of Article 7. This would be true even if the income is sourced in a third State.

There is an exception to this general rule with respect to income a resident of a Contracting State derives from real property located outside the other Contracting State (whether in the first-mentioned Contracting State or in a third State) that is attributable to the resident's permanent establishment or fixed base in the other Contracting State. In such a case, only the first-mentioned Contracting State (i.e., the State of residence of the person deriving the income) and not the host State of the permanent establishment or fixed base may tax that income. This special rule for foreign-situs property is consistent with the general rule, also reflected in Article 6 (Income from Immovable Property (Real Property)), that only the situs and residence States may tax real property and real property income. Even if such property is part of the property of a permanent establishment or fixed base in a Contracting State, that State may not tax it if neither the situs of the property nor the residence of the owner is in that State.

The provisions of paragraph 8 of Article 7 (Business Profits) apply to this paragraph. For example, other income that is attributable to a permanent establishment or a fixed base and that accrues during the existence of the permanent establishment or fixed base, but is received after the permanent establishment or fixed base no longer exists, remains taxable under the provisions of Articles 7 (Business Profits) or 14 (Independent Personal Services), respectively, and not under this Article.

Paragraph 3

Paragraph 3 is not found in the U.S. or OECD Models. It is taken from the U.N. Model. It modifies the general rule of paragraph 1. It provides that, notwithstanding paragraphs 1 and 2, items of income of a resident of a Contracting State not dealt with in the other articles of the Convention and arising in the other Contracting State, may also be taxed in that other Contracting State. Thus, gambling income of a resident of the United States that arises in Venezuela may be taxed both in the United States and in Venezuela. Paragraph 1, therefore, provides exclusive residence-based taxation only to income of a resident of a Contracting State that does not arise in the other Contracting State.

Relation to other articles

This Article is subject to the saving clause of paragraph 4 of Article 1 (Personal Scope). Thus, the United States may tax the income of a resident of Venezuela that is not dealt with elsewhere in the Convention, if that resident is a citizen of the United States. The Article is also subject to the provisions of Article 17 (Limitation on Benefits). Thus, if a resident of Venezuela earns income that falls within the scope of paragraph 1 of Article 21, but that is taxable by the United States under U.S. law, the income would be exempt from U.S. tax under the provisions of Article 21 only if the resident satisfies one of the tests of Article 18 for entitlement to benefits.

ARTICLE 23 (CAPITAL)

This Article specifies the circumstances in which a Contracting State may impose tax on capital owned by a resident of the other Contracting State. While absent from the U.S. Model, the inclusion of a Capital Article is appropriate because of Venezuela's Business Assets Tax (BAT), which serves as a type of alternative minimum tax. The BAT is a covered tax for Venezuela under subparagraph 1 (a) of Article 2 (Taxes Covered). However, it should be noted that in accordance with subparagraph 3 (a) of Article 24 (Relief from Double Taxation) the Convention does not require the United States to allow foreign tax credits for Venezuelan BAT paid. Since the United States does not impose taxes on capital, the only capital taxes covered by the Convention is the BAT of Venezuela. Thus, although the Article is drafted in a reciprocal manner, its provisions are relevant only for the imposition of the BAT of Venezuela. The explanation which follows will be from the perspective of Venezuela as the taxing State.

The Article provides the general rule in paragraph 4 that, except as provided elsewhere in the Article, capital owned by a resident of a Contracting State may be taxed only by that Contracting State. Thus, in general, Venezuela cannot tax a resident of the United States on capital owned by that resident. Exceptions to this general rule are provided in paragraphs 1, 2 and 3.

Paragraph 1 provides that capital represented by real property (as defined in Article 6 (Income from Real Property (Immovable Property)) which is owned by a U.S. resident and located in Venezuela may be taxed by Venezuela. Under paragraph 2, capital which is represented by personal property which is part of the business property of a permanent establishment maintained by a U.S. resident in Venezuela or pertains to a fixed base maintained in Venezuela by a U.S. resident may be taxed by Venezuela. Paragraph 3 deals with capital represented by ships, aircraft or containers that are owned by a U.S. resident, and are operated in international traffic and with other personal property pertaining to the operation of such ships, aircraft or containers. Under the paragraph, such capital is taxable only in the United States.

Thus, the capital to which each of paragraphs 1, 2 and 3 of the Article relate is subject to taxation in the same manner as is income from such capital under Articles 6 (Income from Real Property (Immovable Property)), 7 (Business Profits), 8 (Shipping and Air Transport) and 13 (Gains) of the Convention.

ARTICLE 24 (RELIEF FROM DOUBLE TAXATION)

Paragraph 1

Paragraph 1 confirms the understanding that the Contracting States shall avoid double taxation in accordance with the paragraphs of this Article. Paragraphs 2 and 3 describe the manner in which each Contracting State undertakes to relieve double taxation. The United States uses the foreign tax credit method under its internal law, and by treaty. Venezuela employs a broad exemption method under its internal law and may use either the exemption or foreign tax credit methods under this Convention.

Paragraph 2

Venezuela agrees in paragraph 2 to allow to its residents relief from double taxation of income derived by that resident which, in accordance with the provisions of the Convention, may be taxed in the United States. This relief is granted in accordance with, and subject to the limitations of the law of Venezuela, as they may be amended over time, so long as the general principle of the Article, i.e., the allowance of relief, is retained. The primary method of avoiding double taxation used by Venezuela, under its territorial-based system of taxation, is a broad exemption of foreign source income from Venezuelan tax. This is the method provided in paragraph 2 (a). Subparagraph 2 (b) would apply in the case that Venezuela adopts a worldwide system of taxation, under which it would avoid double taxation by granting foreign tax credits.

Paragraph 3

The United States agrees, in paragraph 3, to allow to its citizens and residents a credit against U.S. tax for income taxes paid or accrued to Venezuela.

The credit under the Convention is allowed in accordance with the provisions and subject to the limitations of U.S. law, as that law may be amended over time, so long as the general principle of this Article, i.e., the allowance of a credit, is retained. Thus, although the Convention provides for a foreign tax credit, the terms of the credit are determined by the provisions, at the time a credit is given, of the U.S. statutory credit.

As indicated, the U.S. credit under the Convention is subject to the various limitations of U.S. law (see Code sections 901 - 908). For example, the credit against U.S. tax generally is limited to the amount of U.S. tax due with respect to net foreign source income within the relevant foreign tax credit limitation category (see, Code section 904(a) and (d)), and the dollar amount of the credit is determined in accordance with U.S. currency translation rules (see, e.g., Code section 986). Similarly, U.S. law applies to determine carryover periods for excess credits and other inter-year adjustments. When the alternative minimum tax is due, the alternative minimum tax foreign tax credit generally is limited in accordance with U.S. law to 90 percent of alternative minimum tax liability. Furthermore, nothing in the Convention prevents the limitation of the U.S. credit from being applied on a per-country basis (should internal law be changed), an overall basis, or to particular categories of income (see, e.g., Code section 865(h)).

Subparagraph (b) provides for a deemed-paid credit, consistent with section 902 of the Code, to a U.S. corporation in respect of dividends received from a corporation resident in Venezuela of which the U.S. corporation owns at least 10 percent of the voting stock. This credit is for the tax paid by the corporation of Venezuela on the profits out of which the dividends are considered paid.

Relation to other articles

By virtue of the exceptions in subparagraph 5(a) of Article 1 this Article is not subject to the saving clause of paragraph 4 of Article 1 (General Scope). Thus, the United States will allow a credit to its citizens and residents in accordance with the Article, even if such credit were to provide a benefit not available under the Code.

ARTICLE 25 (NON-DISCRIMINATION)

This Article assures that nationals of a Contracting State, in the case of paragraph 1, and residents of a Contracting State, in the case of paragraphs 2, 4 and 5, will not be subject, directly or indirectly, to discriminatory taxation in the other Contracting State. For this purpose, non-discrimination means providing national treatment. Not all differences in tax treatment, either as between nationals of the two States, or between residents of the two States, are violations of this national treatment standard. Rather, the national treatment obligation of this Article applies only if the nationals or residents of the two States are comparably situated.

Each of the relevant paragraphs of the Article provides that two persons that are comparably situated must be treated similarly. Although the actual words differ from paragraph to paragraph (e.g., the Protocol's paragraph 17, which clarifies paragraph 1, refers to two nationals "in the same circumstances," paragraph 2 refers to two enterprises "carrying on the same activities" and paragraph 5 refers to two enterprises which are "similarly situated"), the common underlying premise is that if the difference in treatment is directly related to a tax-relevant difference in the situations of the domestic and foreign persons being compared, that difference is not to be treated as discriminatory (e.g., if one person is taxable in a Contracting State on worldwide income and the other is not, or tax may be collectible from one person at a later stage, but not from the other, distinctions in treatment would be justified under paragraph 1). Other examples of such factors that can lead to non-discriminatory differences in treatment will be noted in the discussions of each paragraph.

The operative paragraphs of the Article also use different language to identify the kinds of differences in taxation treatment that will be considered discriminatory. For example, paragraphs 1 and 5 speak of "any taxation or any requirement connected therewith that is other or more burdensome," while paragraph 2 specifies that a tax "shall not be less favorably levied." Regardless of these differences in language, only differences in tax treatment that materially disadvantage the foreign person relative to the domestic person are properly the subject of the Article.

Paragraph 1

Paragraph 1 provides that a national of one Contracting State may not be subject to taxation or connected requirements in the other Contracting State that are other or more burdensome than the taxes and connected requirements imposed upon a national of that other State in the same circumstances. This is consistent with the OECD Model, while differing slightly from the U.S. Model, which refers only to taxes and other requirements that are more burdensome than the taxes and connected requirements imposed upon a national of that other State in the same circumstances.

As noted above, whether or not the two persons are both taxable on worldwide income is a significant circumstance for this purpose. The 1992 revision of the OECD Model added after the words "in the same circumstances," the phrase "in particular with respect to residence," reflecting the fact that under most countries' laws residents are taxable on worldwide income and nonresidents are not. Since in the United States nonresident citizens are also taxable on worldwide income, the Convention's Protocol paragraph 17 expands the phrase to refer, not to residence, but to taxation on worldwide income. The underlying concept, however, is essentially the same as in the OECD Model.

A national of a Contracting State is afforded protection under this paragraph even if the national is not a resident of either Contracting State. Thus, a U.S. citizen who is resident in a third country is entitled, under this paragraph, to the same treatment in Venezuela as a national of Venezuela who is in similar circumstances (i.e., presumably one who is resident in a third State). The term "national" in relation to a Contracting State is defined in subparagraph 1(g) of Article 3 (General Definitions).

Because the relevant circumstances referred to in the paragraph relate, among other things, to taxation on worldwide income, paragraph 1 does not obligate the United States to apply the same taxing regime to a national of Venezuela who is not resident in the United States and a U.S. national who is not resident in the United States. United States citizens who are not residents of the United States but who are, nevertheless, subject to United States tax on their worldwide income are not in the same circumstances with respect to United States taxation as citizens of Venezuela who are not United States residents. Thus, for example, Article 25 and the understanding stated in Protocol paragraph 17 would not entitle a national of Venezuela resident in a third country to taxation at graduated rates of U.S. source dividends or other investment income that applies to a U.S. citizen resident in the same third country.

The scope of paragraph 1 in this Convention and the U.S. Model is broader than that in the 1981 Model, because of the expanded definition of the term "national" in Article 3 (General Definitions). In order to conform the Convention's definition to that in the OECD Model, the definition of "national" extends beyond individuals possessing the nationality of a Contracting State to also cover juridical persons and other entities such as Venezuelan *"entidades"* and *"colectividades"* that are nationals of a Contracting State as well.

Paragraph 2

Paragraph 2 of the Article, like the comparable paragraph in the OECD Model, provides that a Contracting State may not tax a permanent establishment of an enterprise of the other Contracting State less favorably than an enterprise of that first-mentioned State that is carrying on the same activities. This provision, however, does not obligate a Contracting State to grant to a resident of the other Contracting State any tax allowances, reliefs, etc., that it grants to its own residents on account of their civil status or family responsibilities. Thus, if a sole proprietor who is a resident of Venezuela has a permanent establishment in the United States, in assessing income tax on the profits attributable to the permanent establishment, the United States is not obligated to allow to the resident of Venezuela the personal allowances for himself and his family that he would be permitted to take if the permanent establishment were a sole proprietorship owned and operated by a U.S. resident, despite the fact that the individual income tax rates would apply.

The fact that a U.S. permanent establishment of an enterprise of Venezuela is subject to U.S. tax only on income that is attributable to the permanent establishment, while a U.S. corporation engaged in the same activities is taxable on its worldwide income is not, in itself, a sufficient difference to deny national treatment to the permanent establishment. There are cases, however, where the two enterprises would not be similarly situated and differences in treatment may be warranted. For instance, it would not be a violation of the non-discrimination protection of paragraph 2 to require the foreign enterprise to provide information in a reasonable manner that may be different from the information requirements imposed on a resident enterprise, because information may not be as readily available to the Internal Revenue Service from a foreign as from a domestic enterprise. Similarly, it would not be a violation of paragraph 2 to impose penalties on persons who fail to comply with such a requirement (see, e.g., sections 874(a) and 882(c)(2)). Further, a determination that income and expenses have been attributed or allocated to a permanent establishment in conformity with the principles of Article 7 (Business Profits) implies that the attribution or allocation was not discriminatory.

Section 1446 of the Code imposes on any partnership with income that is effectively connected with a U.S. trade or business the obligation to withhold tax on amounts allocable to a foreign partner. In the context of the Convention, this obligation applies with respect to a share of the partnership income of a partner resident in the other Contracting State, and attributable to a U.S. permanent establishment. There is no similar obligation with respect to the distributive shares of U.S. resident partners. It is understood, however, that this distinction is not a form of discrimination within the meaning of paragraph 2 of the Article. No distinction is made between U.S. and non-U.S. partnerships, since the law requires that partnerships of both U.S. and non-U.S. domicile withhold tax in respect of the partnership shares of non-U.S. partners. Furthermore, in distinguishing between U.S. and non-U.S. partners, the requirement to withhold on the non-U.S. but not the U.S. partner's share is not discriminatory taxation, but, like other withholding on nonresident aliens, is merely a reasonable method for the collection of tax from persons who are not continually present in the United States, and as to whom it otherwise may be difficult for the United States to enforce its tax jurisdiction. If tax has been over-withheld, the partner can, as in other cases of over- withholding, file for a refund. (The relationship between paragraph 2 and the imposition of the branch tax is dealt with below in the discussion of paragraph 3.)

Paragraph 3

Paragraph 3 of the Article confirms that no provision of the Article will prevent either Contracting State from imposing the branch taxes described in Article 11A (Branch Tax). Since imposition of the branch taxes under the Convention is specifically sanctioned by Article 11A, its imposition could not be precluded by Article 25, even without paragraph 3. Under the generally accepted rule of construction that the specific takes precedence over the more general, the specific branch tax provisions of Article 11A would take precedence over the more general national treatment provision of Article 25.

Paragraph 4

Paragraph 4 prohibits discrimination in the allowance of deductions. When an enterprise of a Contracting State pays interest, royalties or other disbursements to a resident of the other Contracting State, the first-mentioned Contracting State must allow a deduction for those payments in computing the taxable profits of the enterprise as if the payment had been made under the same conditions to a resident of the first-mentioned Contracting State. An exception to this rule is provided for cases where the provisions of paragraph 1 of Article 9 (Associated Enterprises), paragraph 8 of Article 11 (Interest) or paragraph 6 of Article 12 (Royalties) apply, because in these situations, the related parties have entered into transactions on a non-arm's-length basis. This exception would include the denial or deferral of certain interest deductions under Code section 163(j).

The term "other disbursements" is understood to include a reasonable allocation of executive and general administrative expenses, research and development expenses and other expenses incurred for the benefit of a group of related persons that includes the person incurring the expense.

Paragraph 4 also provides that any debts of an enterprise of a Contracting State to a resident of the other Contracting State are deductible in the first-mentioned Contracting State for computing the capital tax of the enterprise under the same conditions as if the debt had been contracted to a resident of the first-mentioned Contracting State. Even though, for general purposes, the only capital tax covered by the Convention is Venezuela's business assets tax, under paragraph 6 of this Article, the non-discrimination provisions apply to all taxes levied in both Contracting States, at all levels of government. Thus, this provision may be relevant for both States, as many local governments in the United States impose capital taxes.

Paragraph 5

Paragraph 5 requires that a Contracting State not impose other or more burdensome taxation or connected requirements on an enterprise of that State that is wholly or partly owned or controlled, directly or indirectly, by one or more residents of the other Contracting State, than the taxation or connected requirements that it imposes on other similar enterprises of that first-mentioned Contracting State. For this purpose it is understood that "similar" refers to similar activities or ownership of the enterprise.

This rule, like all non-discrimination provisions, does not prohibit differing treatment of entities that are in differing circumstances. Rather, a protected enterprise is only required to be treated in the same manner as other enterprises that, from the point of view of the application of the tax law, are in substantially similar circumstances both in law and in fact. The taxation of a distributing corporation under section 367(e) on an applicable distribution to foreign shareholders does not violate paragraph 4 of the Article because a foreign-owned corporation is not similar to a domestically-owned corporation that is accorded nonrecognition treatment under sections 337 and 355.

For the reasons given above in connection with the discussion of paragraph 2 of the Article, it is also understood that the provision in section 1446 of the Code for withholding of tax on non-U.S. partners does not violate paragraph 4 of the Article.

It is further understood that the ineligibility of a U.S. corporation with nonresident alien shareholders to make an election to be an "S" corporation does not violate paragraph 4 of the Article. If a corporation elects to be an S corporation (requiring 75 or fewer shareholders), it is generally not subject to income tax and the shareholders take into account their pro rata shares of the corporation's items of income, loss, deduction or credit. (The purpose of the provision is to allow an individual or small group of individuals to conduct business in corporate form while paying taxes at individual rates as if the business were conducted directly.) A nonresident alien does not pay U.S. tax on a net basis, and, thus, does not generally take into account items of loss, deduction or credit. Thus, the S corporation provisions do not exclude corporations with nonresident alien shareholders because such shareholders are foreign, but only because they are not net-basis taxpayers. Similarly, the provisions exclude corporations with other types of shareholders where the purpose of the provisions cannot be fulfilled or their mechanics implemented. For example, corporations with corporate shareholders are excluded because the purpose of the provisions to permit individuals to conduct a business in corporate form at individual tax rates would not be furthered by their inclusion.

Paragraph 6

As noted above, notwithstanding the specification in Article 2 (Taxes Covered) of taxes covered by the Convention for general purposes, for purposes of providing non-discrimination protection this Article applies to taxes of every kind and description imposed by a Contracting State or a political subdivision or local authority thereof. Customs duties are not considered to be taxes for this purpose.

Relation to other articles

The saving clause of paragraph 4 of Article 1 (General Scope) does not apply to this Article, by virtue of the exceptions in paragraph 5(a) of Article 1. Thus, for example, a U.S. citizen who is a resident of Venezuela may claim benefits in the United States under this Article.

Nationals of a Contracting State may claim the benefits of paragraph 1 regardless of whether they are entitled to benefits under Article 17 (Limitation on Benefits), because that paragraph applies to nationals and not residents. They may not claim the benefits of the other paragraphs of this Article with respect to an item of income unless they are generally entitled to treaty benefits with respect to that income under a provision of Article 17.

ARTICLE 26 (MUTUAL AGREEMENT PROCEDURE)

This Article provides the mechanism for taxpayers to bring to the attention of the Contracting States' competent authorities issues and problems that may arise under the Convention. It also provides a mechanism for cooperation between the competent authorities of the Contracting States to resolve disputes and clarify issues that may arise under the Convention and to resolve cases of double taxation not provided for in the Convention. The competent authorities of the two Contracting States are identified in paragraph 1(i) of Article 3 (General Definitions).

Paragraph 1

This paragraph provides that where a resident of a Contracting State considers that the actions of one or both Contracting States will result in taxation that is not in accordance with the Convention he may present his case to the competent authority of either Contracting State. This is consistent with paragraph 16 of the OECD Commentary to Article 25, which suggests that countries may agree to allow a case to be brought to either competent authority. Because there seems to be no apparent reason why a resident of a Contracting State must take its case to the competent authority of its State of residence and not to that of the partner, the Convention adopts the approach suggested in the OECD Commentary. Under this approach, a U.S. permanent establishment of a corporation resident in Venezuela that faces inconsistent treatment in the two countries would be able to bring its complaint to the competent authority in either Contracting State.

Although the typical cases brought under this paragraph will involve economic double taxation arising from transfer pricing adjustments, the scope of this paragraph is not limited to such cases. For example, if a Contracting State treats income derived by a company resident in the other Contracting State as attributable to a permanent establishment in the first-mentioned Contracting State, and the resident believes that the income is not attributable to a permanent establishment, or that no permanent establishment exists, the resident may bring a complaint under paragraph 1 to the competent authority of either Contracting State.

It is not necessary for a person bringing a complaint first to have exhausted the remedies provided under the national laws of the Contracting States before presenting a case to the competent authorities, nor does the fact that the statute of limitations may have passed for seeking a refund preclude bringing a case to the competent authority. Like the U.S. Model, but unlike the OECD Model, no time limit is provided within which a case must be brought.

Paragraph 2

This paragraph instructs the competent authorities in dealing with cases brought by taxpayers under paragraph 1. It provides that if the competent authority of the Contracting State to which the case is presented judges the case to have merit, and cannot reach a unilateral solution, it shall seek an agreement with the competent authority of the other Contracting State pursuant to which taxation not in accordance with the Convention will be avoided. In a deviation from the U.S. Model, paragraph 2 states that, provided that the statute of limitations has been interrupted in accordance with the steps designated under domestic law, any agreement is to be implemented even if such implementation otherwise would be barred by the statute of limitations or by some other procedural limitation, such as a closing agreement. In a case where the taxpayer has entered a closing agreement (or other written settlement) with the United States prior to bringing a case to the competent authorities, the U.S. competent authority will endeavor only to obtain a correlative adjustment from the other Contracting State. See, Rev. Proc. 96-13, 1996-3 I.R.B. 31, section 7.05. Because, as specified in paragraph 2 of Article 1 (General Scope), the

Convention cannot operate to increase a taxpayer's liability, time or other procedural limitations can be overridden only for the purpose of making refunds and not to impose additional tax.

Paragraph 3

Paragraph 3 authorizes the competent authorities to resolve difficulties or doubts that may arise as to the application or interpretation of the Convention. The paragraph includes a non-exhaustive list of examples of the kinds of matters about which the competent authorities may reach agreement. This list is purely illustrative; it does not grant any authority that is not implicitly present as a result of the introductory sentence of paragraph 3. The competent authorities may, for example, agree to the same allocation of income, deductions, credits or allowances between an enterprise in one Contracting State and its permanent establishment in the other (subparagraph (a)) or between persons (subparagraph (b)). These allocations are to be made in accordance with the arm's length principle underlying Article 7 (Business Profits) and Article 9 (Associated Enterprises). Agreements reached under these subparagraphs may include agreement on a methodology for determining an appropriate transfer price, common treatment of a taxpayer's cost sharing arrangement, or upon an acceptable range of results under that methodology.

As indicated in subparagraphs (c), (d), (e) and (f), the competent authorities also may agree to settle a variety of conflicting applications of the Convention. They may agree to characterize particular items of income in the same way (subparagraph (c)), to apply the same source rules to particular items of income(subparagraph (d)), to adopt a common meaning of a term (subparagraph (e)).

Subparagraph (f) authorizes the competent authorities to increase any dollar amounts referred to in the Convention to reflect economic and monetary developments. Under the Convention, this refers to Articles 18 (Artistes and Sportsmen) and 21 (Students, Trainees, Teachers and Researchers). The rule under subparagraph (f) is intended to operate as follows: if, for example, after the Convention has been in force for some time, inflation rates have been such as to make the $6,000 exemption threshold for entertainers in Article 18 unrealistically low in terms of the original objectives intended in setting the threshold, the competent authorities may agree to a higher threshold without the need for formal amendment to the treaty and ratification by the Contracting States. This authority can be exercised, however, only to the extent necessary to restore those original objectives. This provision can be applied only to the benefit of taxpayers, i.e., only to increase thresholds, not to reduce them.

Subparagraph (g) makes clear that the competent authorities can agree to the common application, consistent with the objective of avoiding double taxation, of procedural provisions of the internal laws of the Contracting States, including those regarding penalties, fines and interest.

Since the list under paragraph 3 is not exhaustive, the competent authorities may reach agreement on issues not enumerated in paragraph 3 if necessary to avoid double taxation. For example, the competent authorities may seek agreement on a uniform set of standards for the use of exchange rates, or agree on consistent timing of gain recognition with respect to a transaction to the extent necessary to avoid double taxation. Agreements reached by the competent authorities under paragraph 3 need not conform to the internal law provisions of either Contracting State.

Finally, paragraph 3 authorizes the competent authorities to consult for the purpose of eliminating double taxation in cases not provided for in the Convention and to resolve any difficulties or doubts arising as to the interpretation or application of the Convention. This provision is intended to permit the competent authorities to implement the treaty in particular cases in a manner that is consistent with its expressed general purposes. It permits the competent authorities to deal with cases that are within the spirit of the provisions but that are not specifically covered. An example of such a case might be double taxation arising from a transfer pricing adjustment between two permanent establishments of a third-country resident, one in the United States and one in Venezuela. Since no resident of a Contracting State is involved in the case, the Convention does not apply, but the competent authorities nevertheless may use the authority of the Convention to prevent the double taxation.

Paragraph 4

Paragraph 4 provides that the competent authorities may communicate with each other for the purpose of reaching an agreement. This makes clear that the competent authorities of the two Contracting States may communicate without going through diplomatic channels. Such communication may be in various forms, including, where appropriate, through face-to-face meetings of the competent authorities or their representatives.

Other issues

Treaty effective dates and termination in relation to competent authority dispute resolution

A case may be raised by a taxpayer under a treaty with respect to a year for which a treaty was in force after the treaty has been terminated. In such a case the ability of the competent authorities to act is limited. They may not exchange confidential information, nor may they reach a solution that varies from that specified in its law.

A case also may be brought to a competent authority under a treaty that is in force, but with respect to a year prior to the entry into force of the treaty. The scope of the competent authorities to address such a case is not constrained by the fact that the treaty was not in force when the transactions at issue occurred, and the competent authorities have available to them the full range of remedies afforded under this Article.

Triangular competent authority solutions

International tax cases may involve more than two taxing jurisdictions (e.g., transactions among a parent corporation resident in country A and its subsidiaries resident in countries B and C). As long as there is a complete network of treaties among the three countries, it should be possible, under the full combination of bilateral authorities, for the competent authorities of the three States to work together on a three-sided solution. Although country A may not be able to give information received under Article 27 (Exchange of Information) from country B to the authorities of country C, if the competent authorities of the three countries are working together, it should not be a problem for them to arrange for the authorities of country B to give the necessary information directly to the tax authorities of country C, as well as to those of country A. Each bilateral part of the trilateral solution must, of course, not exceed the scope of the authority of the competent authorities under the relevant bilateral treaty.

Relation to other articles

This Article is not subject to the saving clause of paragraph 4 of Article 1 (General Scope) by virtue of the exceptions in paragraph 5(a) of that Article. Thus, rules, definitions, procedures, etc. that are agreed upon by the competent authorities under this Article may be applied by the United States with respect to its citizens and residents even if they differ from the comparable Code provisions. Similarly, as indicated above, U.S. law may be overridden to provide refunds of tax to a U.S. citizen or resident under this Article. A person may seek relief under Article 26 regardless of whether he is generally entitled to benefits under Article 17 (Limitation on Benefits). As in all other cases, the competent authority is vested with the discretion to decide whether the claim for relief is justified.

ARTICLE 27 (EXCHANGE OF INFORMATION)

Paragraph 1

This Article provides for the exchange of information between the competent authorities of the Contracting States. The information to be exchanged is that which is necessary for carrying out the provisions of the Convention or the domestic laws of the United States or of Venezuela concerning the taxes covered by the Convention. The reference to information that is "necessary" is consistent with the OECD Model, and while the U.S. Model refers to information that is "relevant," the terms consistently have been interpreted as being equivalent, and as not requiring a requesting State to demonstrate that it would be unable to enforce its tax laws unless it obtained a particular item of information. Therefore, it should not be interpreted that "necessary" creates a higher threshold than "relevant."

The taxes covered by the Convention for purposes of this Article constitute a broader category of taxes than those referred to in Article 2 (Taxes Covered). As provided in paragraph 4, for purposes of exchange of information, covered taxes include all taxes imposed by the Contracting States. Exchange of information with respect to domestic law is authorized insofar as the taxation under those domestic laws is not contrary to the Convention. Thus, for example, information may be exchanged with respect to a covered tax, even if the transaction to which the information relates is a purely domestic transaction in the requesting State and, therefore, the exchange is not made for the purpose of carrying out the Convention.

An example of such a case is provided in the OECD Commentary: A company resident in the United States and a company resident in Venezuela transact business between themselves through a third-country resident company. Neither Contracting State has a treaty with the third State. In order to enforce their internal laws with respect to transactions of their residents with the third-country company (since there is no relevant treaty in force), the Contracting State may exchange information regarding the prices that their residents paid in their transactions with the third-country resident.

Paragraph 1 states that information exchange is not restricted by Article 1 (General Scope). Accordingly, information may be requested and provided under this Article with respect to persons who are not residents of either Contracting State. For example, if a third-country resident has a permanent establishment in Venezuela which engages in transactions with a U.S. enterprise, the United States could request information with respect to that permanent establishment, even though it is not a resident of either Contracting State. Similarly, if a third--country resident maintains a bank account in Venezuela, and the Internal Revenue Service has reason to believe that funds in that account should have been reported for U.S. tax purposes but have not been so reported, information can be requested from Venezuela with respect to that person's account.

Paragraph 1 also provides assurances that any information exchanged will be treated as secret, subject to the same disclosure constraints as information obtained under the laws of the requesting State. Information received may be disclosed only to persons, including courts and administrative bodies, involved with the assessment, collection, enforcement or prosecution in respect of the taxes to which the information relates, or to persons involved with the administration of these taxes or with the oversight of such activities. The information must be used by these persons in connection with these designated functions. Persons in the United States involved with the oversight of the administration of taxes include legislative bodies, such as the tax-writing committees of Congress and the General Accounting Office. Information received by these bodies must be for use in the performance of their role in overseeing the administration of U.S. tax laws. Information received may be disclosed in public court proceedings or in judicial decisions.

The Article authorizes the competent authorities to exchange information on a routine basis, on request in relation to a specific case, or spontaneously. It is contemplated that the Contracting States will utilize this authority to engage in all of these forms of information exchange, as appropriate.

Paragraph 2

Paragraph 2 is identical to paragraph 2 of Article 26 of the OECD Model. It provides that the obligations undertaken in paragraph 1 to exchange information do not require a Contracting State to carry out administrative measures that are at variance with the laws or administrative practice of either State. Nor is a Contracting State required to supply information not obtainable under the laws or administrative practice of either State, or to disclose trade secrets or other information, the disclosure of which would be contrary to public policy. Thus, a requesting State may be denied information from the other State if the information would be obtained pursuant to procedures or measures that are broader than those available in the requesting State.

While paragraph 2 states conditions under which a Contracting State is not obligated to comply with a request from the other Contracting State for information, the requested State is not precluded from providing such information, and may, at its discretion, do so subject to the limitations of its internal law.

Paragraph 3

Paragraph 3 does not have an analog in the OECD Model. It provides that when information is requested by a Contracting State in accordance with this Article, the other Contracting State is obligated to obtain the requested information as if the tax in question were the tax of the requested State, even if that State has no direct tax interest in the case to which the request relates. The OECD Model does not state explicitly in the Article that the requested State is obligated to respond to a request even if it does not have a direct tax interest in the information. The OECD Commentary, however, makes clear that this is to be understood as implicit in the OECD Model. (See paragraph 16 of the OECD Commentary to Article 26.)

The Convention does not include the first sentence of paragraph 3 of the U.S. Model dealing with bank secrecy rules. Paragraph 19 of the Protocol clarifies that the competent authorities of both Contracting States have the necessary authority under their domestic laws to comply with the provisions of this Article, and specifically to obtain information held by persons other than taxpayers, including information held by financial institutions, agents and trustees, so such sentence was not necessary.

Paragraph 3 further provides that the requesting State may specify the form in which information is to be provided (e.g., depositions of witnesses and authenticated copies of original documents) so that the information is usable in the judicial proceedings of the requesting State. The requested State should, if possible, provide the information in the form requested to the same extent that it can obtain information in that form under its own laws and administrative practices with respect to its own taxes.

Paragraph 4

As noted above in the discussion of paragraph 1, the exchange of information provisions of the Convention apply to all taxes imposed by a Contracting State, not just to those taxes designated as covered taxes under Article 2 (Taxes Covered). The U.S. competent authority may, therefore, request information for purposes of, for example, estate and gift taxes or federal excise taxes.

Treaty effective dates and termination in relation to exchange of information

A tax administration may seek information with respect to a year for which a treaty was in force after the treaty has been terminated. In such a case the ability of the other tax administration to act is limited. The treaty no longer provides authority for the tax administrations to exchange confidential information. They may only exchange information pursuant to domestic law.

ARTICLE 28 (DIPLOMATIC AGENTS AND CONSULAR OFFICERS)

This Article confirms that any fiscal privileges to which diplomatic or consular officials are entitled under general provisions of international law or under special agreements will apply notwithstanding any provisions to the contrary in the Convention. The agreements referred to include any bilateral agreements, such as consular conventions, that affect the taxation of diplomats and consular officials and any multilateral agreements dealing with these issues, such as the Vienna Convention on Diplomatic Relations and the Vienna Convention on Consular Relations. The U.S. generally adheres to the latter because its terms are consistent with customary international law.

The Article does not independently provide any benefits to diplomatic agents and consular officers. Article 20 (Government Service) does so, as do Code section 893 and a number of bilateral and multilateral agreements. In the event that there is a conflict between the tax treaty and international law or such other treaties, under which the diplomatic agent or consular official is entitled to greater benefits under the latter, the latter laws or agreements shall have precedence. Conversely, if the tax treaty confers a greater benefit than another agreement, the affected person could claim the benefit of the tax treaty.

Pursuant to subparagraph 5(b) of Article 1, the saving clause of paragraph 4 of Article 1 (General Scope) does not apply to override any benefits of this Article available to an individual who is neither a citizen of the United States nor has immigrant status in the United States.

ARTICLE 29 (ENTRY INTO FORCE)

This Article contains the rules for bringing the Convention into force and giving effect to its provisions.

Paragraph 1

Paragraph 1 provides for the ratification of the Convention by both Contracting States according to their constitutional and statutory requirements. Each State must notify the other through the diplomatic channel as soon as its requirements for ratification have been complied with. Paragraph 1 also requires that instruments of ratification accompany the notifications.

In the United States, the process leading to ratification and entry into force is as follows: Once a treaty has been signed by authorized representatives of the two Contracting States, the Department of State sends the treaty to the President who formally transmits it to the Senate for its advice and consent to ratification, which requires approval by two-thirds of the Senators present and voting. Prior to this vote, however, it generally has been the practice for the Senate Committee on Foreign Relations to hold hearings on the treaty and make a recommendation regarding its approval to the full Senate. Both Government and private sector witnesses may testify at these hearings. After receiving the Senate's advice and consent to ratification, the treaty is returned to the President for his signature on the ratification document. The President's signature on the document completes the process in the United States.

Paragraph 2

Paragraph 2 provides that the Convention will enter into force on the date on which the second of the two notifications of the completion of ratification requirements and accompanying instrument of ratification has been received. The date on which a treaty enters into force is not necessarily the date on which its provisions take effect. Paragraph 2, therefore, also contains rules that determine when the provisions of the treaty will have effect. Under paragraph 2(a), the Convention will have effect with respect to taxes withheld at source (principally dividends, interest and royalties) for amounts paid or credited on or after January 1 of the year following the date on which the Convention enters into force. For example, if instruments of ratification are exchanged on April 25 of a given year, the withholding rates specified in paragraph 2 of Article 10 (Dividends) would be applicable to any dividends paid or credited on or after January 1 of the following year. If for some reason a withholding agent withholds at a higher rate than that provided by the Convention (perhaps because it was not able to re-program its computers before the payment is made), the beneficial owner of the income may make a claim for refund pursuant to section 1464 of the Code.

Likewise, for all other taxes, paragraph 2(b) specifies that the Convention will have effect for any taxable year or assessment period beginning on or after January 1 of the year following entry into force.

ARTICLE 30 (TERMINATION)

This Article contains the rules for terminating the Convention.

Paragraph 1

Paragraph 1 states that the Convention is to remain in effect indefinitely, unless terminated by one of the Contracting States in accordance with the provisions of Article 30. The Convention may be terminated at any time after the year in which the Convention enters into force, provided that at least six months prior notice of the termination has been given through the diplomatic channel. If such notice of termination is given, subparagraph (a) provides that the provisions of the Convention with respect to withholding at source will cease to have effect on or after January 1 of the year following the date on which the notice is given. Likewise, for other taxes, the Convention will cease to have effect as of taxable periods beginning on or after January 1 of the year following the date on which the notice is given.

Paragraph 2

Paragraph 2 is intended to deal with changes in law of either of the Contracting States that have the effect of changing the application of the Convention in a significant manner or that alter the relationship between the Contracting States. Paragraph 2 provides, first, that, in response to a change in the law of either State, the appropriate authority of either State may request consultations with its counterpart in the other State to determine whether a change in the Convention is appropriate. The "appropriate authorities" may be the Contracting States themselves, communicating through diplomatic channels, or they may be the competent authorities under the Convention, communicating directly. The request for consultations may come either from the authority of the Contracting State making the change in law, or it may come from the authority of the other State. If the authorities determine, on the basis of consultations, that a change in domestic legislation has significantly altered the balance provided by the Convention, they will consult with a view to amending the Convention to restore an appropriate balance. Any such amendment would, of course, require a protocol or new treaty which would be subject to Senate advice and consent to ratification.

Other aspects of Article

A treaty performs certain specific and necessary functions regarding information exchange and mutual agreement. In the case of information exchange the treaty's function is to override confidentiality rules relating to taxpayer information. In the case of mutual agreement its function is to allow competent authorities to modify internal law in order to prevent double taxation and tax avoidance. With respect to the effective termination dates for these aspects of the treaty, therefore, if a treaty is terminated as of January 1 of a given year, no otherwise confidential information can be exchanged after that date, regardless of whether the treaty was in force for the taxable year to which the request relates. Similarly, no mutual agreement departing from internal law can be implemented after that date, regardless of the taxable year to which the agreement relates. Therefore, for the competent authorities to be allowed to exchange otherwise confidential information or to reach a mutual agreement that departs from internal law, a treaty must be in force at the time those actions are taken and any existing competent authority agreement ceases to apply.

Article 30 relates only to unilateral termination of the Convention by a Contracting State. Nothing in that Article should be construed as preventing the Contracting States from concluding a new bilateral agreement, subject to ratification, that supersedes, amends or terminates provisions of the Convention without the six-month notification period.

Customary international law observed by the United States and other countries, as reflected in the Vienna Convention on Treaties, allows termination by one Contracting State at any time in the event of a "material breach" of the agreement by the other Contracting State.

www.ingramcontent.com/pod-product-compliance
Lightning Source LLC
Chambersburg PA
CBHW081226280526
45787CB00006B/2543